What a clear, easy to follow book for all real estate professionals or anyone in running their own business in any niche! Tricia Andreassen is a marketing expert. She makes her principles logical and meaningful through everyday examples. And, she includes many visuals so the reader sees exactly what she's talking about. The best part of her book, I think, are the questionnaires, where the author asks the reader to put the principles to work in their own business lives, so they walk away with a real action plan. I highly recommended Tricia's new book for anyone who wants to take their web marketing strategy to the highest level.

– Carla Cross, CRB, MA
Real Estate Management Specialist, Speaker, Coach
Author of 7 books including, *What They Don't Teach You in Pre-License School*
www.CarlaCross.com

Today most are so busy working IN their business that they often have no time left to work ON their business. Don't miss Tricia Andreassen's book with a comprehensive roadmap to creating differentiation in a crowded marketplace. These skills will be critical to your being positioned as the expert they respect and the resource they need!

– Don Hutson
Co-Author of the NY Times & Wall Street Journal #1 Best-Seller,
The One Minute Entrepreneur, and CEO of U. S. Learning

Today's successful business people must master their unique voice in the marketplace. Tricia's book clearly delineates a step by step process to go from ordinary to extraordinary by adopting the principles of Interfusion Marketing. It's not about the next shiny new app; it's about deliberate and effective strategies that help position you as the "celebrity authority" in your marketplace.

The combination of information and guidance is well thought out and easy to follow. This book is a must for any person in business for themselves willing to propel their production and presence in their market to the next level and beyond.

– Terri Murphy
Author, Speaker, Consultant/eCommunications Specialist
HARNESSING THE POWER OF CONNECTION

Tricia Andreassen is one of the premier leadership and business coaches in the industry. Her track record in helping already successful business leaders build market dominating teams is without peer. She has given us a gift in her new book Interfusion Marketing by taking her no fail approach and making it accessible to anyone who wishes to build an unstoppable business!! I am proof that anyone with a desire to learn and grow their business can do so if they follow Tricia's lead.

– John M. Moore
CEO Certified Executive Leadership & Business Advisor

Tricia Andreassen has written a step-by-step, extremely insightful guide to what it really takes to market and grow a successful business using the latest technology and the tried and true principles that never go out of style. She is exactly right: Marketing is a science. In this book, Tricia explains the science of marketing to you, in a highly motivational, easy-to-implement fashion. I highly recommend her insights and wisdom.

– Andrew Neitlich
Founder and Director, Center for Executive Coaching and Co-Author,
Guerrilla Marketing for Coaches

I love this book! Interfusion Marketing is a must read for any business owner who wants their business to succeed. Andreassen has brought together the best branding, web, social, and print strategies and fused them into a proven plan that will work for your business. If your business is not generating the results you desire, this book has the case studies, the research, and the straight practical advice you need today to achieve great results tomorrow.

– Bernice Ross, CEO
www.RealEstateCoach.com
Nationally Syndicated Columnist, Inman News and CEO of Real Estate Coach
Author of *Real Estate Dough Your Recipe For Real Estate Success!*

Interfusion Marketing is one of the greatest resources I've encountered to help real estate agents or business owners at any level. They will develop and strengthen the marketing facet of their business exponentially! Tricia has created an extremely valuable tool that anyone can use to set themselves apart from the completion and piece together a solid marketing plan for success!

– Linda McLean
Speaker, Certified Coach and
International Best Selling Author of *Next Level Living*

Tricia hit a home run! I was totally impressed with this engaging format, and the easy reading. When you dial into the mindset of your target audience it uncovers the messages, campaigns, scripts and dialogues needed to connect you to your prospect.

– Darryl Davis
Best Selling Author and Speaker

Interfusion Marketing

Unlock The Secret Code To Dominate Your Market

Tricia Andreassen

TAG

TAG Publishing, LLC
2030 S. Milam
Amarillo, TX 79109
www.TAGPublishers.com

Office (806) 373-0114
Fax (806) 373-4004
info@TAGPublishers.com

ISBN: 978-1-934606-60-5

Text: Lloyd Arbour, www.mynewart.com

First Edition

Contents

Acknowledgement

I am so inspired by the people who have crossed my path and shared their insights, knowledge and friendship with me: from my 4th grade teacher who reviewed my first book of poems, to my college professor who edited my first short story, as well as the business people who mentored me in my young twenties. It has built a tremendous collage of experience that has contributed to writing this book.

I have to thank my devoted husband, Kurt, who inspires me every day to grow. It is amazing to have a partner who walks along with you, shares your dreams and always believes in you. Also, thanks to my son Jordan who reminds me every day that he is my most special accomplishment in my life.

Thank you to all my clients and those who contributed with their interviews and insights for this book. Your willingness to give back to others to help them grow their business is golden. Every single one of you shares the same philosophy of giving back and helping others to reach their goals. I am blessed to know you and share the world with you.

Thank you to all my wonderful employees who have worked so many hours to help make this book a reality. Dara Rogers deserves a special acknowledgement. I am so blessed to have such an amazing talent in my organization. She is a living example of one who always has the patience of a saint combined with supreme dedication.

I am grateful for my close friends who have kept my personal flame burning. Linda Mclean, who in 2006 helped me begin crafting my vision, Linda Hall, who always listens and is a powerful sounding board, Kathi King, Coni Myers, Frank Ciraulo, Kristan Cole and so many more that I can't mention you all. You have my unending gratitude.

To my wonderful sister, Karen Storey, who set my path for who I am today. From having me cold call at age 13 to reading Dale Carnegie at 15 and showing me that no dream is unreachable. Thank you – Thank you! I love you Mom and Dad.

Foreword

Many industries are awash with speakers, coaches and gurus. In the real estate industry many of these "experts" fall into two groups. The ones that have done it; they have been in the trenches and know what it's like to conduct a listing presentation or negotiate with a buyer or seller. They have actually "played the game of real estate sales". The second group is made up of the many people in the industry that are simply observers and theorists.

Tricia is one of the few that has done it; she was a successful agent. She then took the step beyond the trenches to touch the lives of hundreds of thousands of agents and business owners with her insight, marketing and success strategies. Tricia takes you on a journey step-by-step through your marketing, brand development and implementation with her revolutionary Interfusion Marketing strategy. The truth is the word "strategy" doesn't give justice to what she has created. This game changing process is really a system. She walks you through, step-by-step to create your unique branding, positioning, target market, specific audience, multiple marketing channels and performance measurement system.

For any business person to have a long term sustainable business they need both an effective marketing system and sales system. In my more than twenty-five years in the real estate industry to find that group of real estate professionals is rare. The relationship aspect of building a business is most frequently used to the exclusion of other marketing systems or relationship marketing systems. In the new technology world we live in, a relationship is not enough.

There is a seismic shift in every business we see. The consumer has more power than ever before. In the real estate industry, for example thirty-two percent of buyers last year, according to NAR, found the agent they used through an online search. Think about that. That was for over 1.6 million buyers units last year. The "relationship" or "referral" didn't come into play in selecting an agent. No matter what business are you in, either real estate or otherwise, it is imperative to understand how to reach today's consumer.

The Interfusion Marketing systems that Tricia has created will insure that you tap into that increasing source of prospects in today's marketplace. As professionals we have to realize that more buyers and sellers are doing research about us in the background. They are using testimonials and survey scores on websites like Google, Zillow, and Yelp for reviews. With real estate you see the explosion of real estate shows on HGTV, DIY Network and others, which empowers buyers to feeling more in control. They have access to information while remaining concealed creating a barrier between you and a prospect. A large volume of DIY consumers feel they know as much as real estate agents and have access to the same exact information. Their primary goal is to remain stealth for as long as possible. Breaking through to these DIY prospects is best done through Tricia's Interfusion Marketing methods.

We must deliver value and position ourselves as an expert. Only then through our marketing and sales strategies can we create that lead and convert it into a client. The transition from prospect to client must incorporate both a "push" and a "pull" strategy to enhance our service and sales numbers. The days of designing a "cool" website with lots of content or tools in our overload society could be doing more harm then good. There has to be strategic thought, lead pathway design, lead follow up and touch systems.

Tricia Andreassen continues to be a top leader in marketing, sales and business for more than 20 years. You have made the right investment in your career! My hope is that you will read this book, study it over and over, mark it up, and keep it handy because of its value as a reference source. There is no question this book will be a profitable investment of your time. It will create the foundation to a more successful marketing strategy that will lead to increased sales, personal satisfaction and wealth.

– Dirk Zeller
Best Selling Author, *Real Estate Sales For Dummies*
CEO of Real Estate Champions

Preface

A few years ago while on vacation, I stopped in at a coffee shop. I powered up my laptop to write that morning before the boys woke up and wanted to go sightseeing. As I got situated with my headphones to zone out to piano music while writing, this gentleman walked over to me and said, "Good morning! What are you working on so intensively?"

His smile made me easily respond. "I am writing a book to help Realtors with their business strategy. I want them to have a marketing plan that connects them to those they specifically want to reach. It's about developing a message and partnering with a brand that will carry over to a website which is designed to build clients for life. Once they have the branding and the website navigation, I then show them how to evangelize the message using different marketing channels such as word of mouth, direct mail, offline and social media. I am really good at helping them pull it all together into a real, workable plan."

He looked at me and said, "You know I am the owner of this shop and I struggle with that all the time. I wish you would write a book for us little guys. We don't know how to make everything work together and the hard part is, we don't know where to start."

He continued to share. "I love making coffee! We grind our own beans and make the coffee fresh so that our customer gets something special. I know they can go to fast food restaurants and get coffee for a buck now, but what we bring is the experience. I want them to feel special when they walk in the door. I want them to smell the coffee and be transported into another world when they sit with us. That is why I have these sofas and comfy chairs, as well as desks like this for you."

He then looked at me and said, "I know you are working on a book for Realtors but, Tricia, I would buy your book today if you could help me with my marketing and show me how to evangelize why we are different."

Even after my vacation, that man's words stayed with me. I thought about how I started my marketing and advertising firm out of the bonus room of my house and then developed it into the successful practice that it is today. For several years, I helped Realtors with their marketing efforts and I could do the same for others. Over time, my marketing methodologies were put into practice with business owners all over the country and included businesses such as air conditioning services, life coaches, executive coaches, landscapers, restaurants and even coffee shops.

A year and a half later, I went back to that coffee shop. It had gone out of business. It made me think, *If only I'd had this book to help him in some way. Maybe he would be in business today.* That idea stayed with me and became my driving passion.

What I uncovered as I worked with so many different types of businesses, is that no matter what the business, there are core similarities; core principles that had to be practiced for any business to establish itself, and then grow and thrive. It was these fundamental ideas that I became passionate in evaluating and revealing in this book. Now you can grow the business of your dreams that fulfills the needs of your core customer base just as I did. You'll consistently grow that business and create a stable, sustainable lifestyle.

SECTION I

Determine Your Unique DNA

SHH! The Secret No One is Telling You!

Have you noticed that no matter what industry you are in, there is a constant buzz about what type of marketing is best for your business? You could spend days on end contemplating the best method to get results: A blog? A website? Dipping your toes into the pool of social media? Sticking with word of mouth and direct mail? The list goes on.

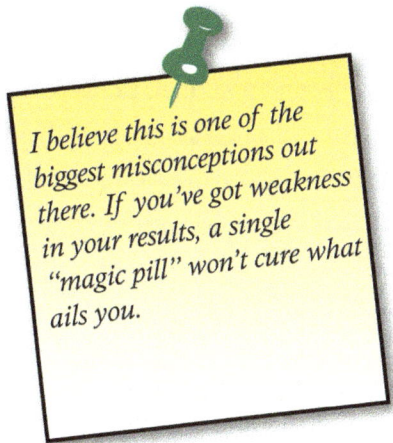

I believe this is one of the biggest misconceptions out there. If you've got weakness in your results, a single "magic pill" won't cure what ails you.

With all those choices, it can be tempting to look for the single "best" marketing technique. How many times have you been told about a miraculous one-size-fits-all solution? We hear it constantly: "Just do this one thing, and you'll get the results you've always wanted!" Everyone wants the fast, big fix.

At one of my recent speaking events, a real estate broker came up to me and said, "Tricia, I heard that websites were a thing of the past and are going away. I don't think I need one."

"Are you kidding me?" I asked. "That would be like saying, 'Well, I'm on Facebook now, so I don't need a business card anymore.'"

So many salespeople and business owners ask me for help with their Internet marketing. I always tell them that in order to get the best results, they need to take the Interfusion approach!

Interfusion (n.)—To blend, combine or add various elements, fusing them together to create a unique new structure.

With **Interfusion Marketing**, you don't just look at one element of your marketing and think that is the only thing you will focus on. Instead, you become mindful of all the various types of marketing that you could be doing, and make sure there's a game plan; a strategy that pulls it all together.

All your marketing must cohesively work together to create a highly effective strategy!

The secret no one tells you is that great marketing is a scientific formula. It is a sprinkling, blending and mixing of your core business ingredients to create the perfect result. It's the formula —the combination of all those ingredients—that will give you what you want out of your marketing and advertising methods.

What's Your DNA?

Have you ever stopped and really looked at someone? I mean really examined their features and thought about how they were created to look a little like each of their parents? It makes you think: We're all so much alike, but yet no two people are completely alike in every way.

This is why I use the DNA analogy when I talk about Interfusion Marketing. It is the combining of foundational elements to create a totally unique outcome. It works the same way DNA

Without those core elements, the genetic code does not work. The same is true for marketing your business. There are core elements that you must start with as a foundation for success. How you use them depends on your own Interfusion Marketing strategy.

works in your body. You see, DNA has three core elements—phosphate, sugar and nitrogen—which are woven together in a complex pattern. It's the weaving together of those individual elements in a unique way that creates the genetic code for every living being. The results are slightly different for everyone, which is why you may have brown eyes while mine are blue.

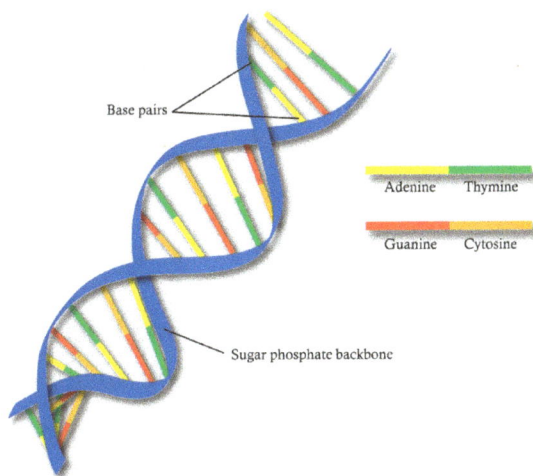

Base pairs

Adenine   Thymine

Guanine   Cytosine

Sugar phosphate backbone

Just think about it: 99.9% of human DNA is exactly the same in all people but that .01% is enough of a difference for us each to look, think and act differently.

So humor me! Think like a scientist, and take a closer look at the core elements of DNA. It's the perfect comparison analogy for creating a solid marketing and business plan.

DNA is made up of three substances: phosphate groups, sugar (dioxyribose) groups and nitrogen bases. Phosphate and sugar combine to make the rails (the sides) of the DNA ladder. The nitrogen bases in DNA are adenine (A), guanine (G), cytosine (C) and thymine (T). A binds with T, while G binds with C.

These bases have to match up (A-T, C-G) for the rungs to connect to the sides of the ladder. When you weave all these elements together, they create the DNA structure of every living thing on Earth.

Compare DNA With Your Business and Marketing Strategy

Phosphate – Phosphate is a core ingredient for DNA, and a great analogy for growing your business. Just go to any garden center and grab a bag of fertilizer. Check the ingredients on the back, and guess what the main ingredient is? Phosphate! This essential element is what makes the flowers bloom.

In this book, you'll learn which marketing pieces you can improve upon (or fertilize), so that your efforts grow and bloom with powerful results.

Sugar – You've heard the expression "you need a sugar high!" and you probably know that sugar is what provides energy to the body. In this case, it equates to your passion, your sexy ads and the compelling things you do to close leads! It's about attracting the type of person you want to work with! Your "sugar high" is the fueling energy behind your business; your mindset and your target market.

What is your own sugar high? What do people crave in your business world? You'll learn to use the law of attraction—"what you focus on expands"—to create the type of business you're excited to work in every day.

Nitrogen – Nitrogen bases are the detailed, consistently blended ingredients of DNA. They must line up exactly (A to T and C to G) to build correctly and create the structure that carries genetic information. These are your everyday actions, the things you do consistently and ways you implement business strategies to create desired results.

We'll talk about forming a sturdy structure through careful planning and strategizing, and then consistently implementing your ideas to build a strong foundation.

Just like the DNA strand, every business should have these core genetics.

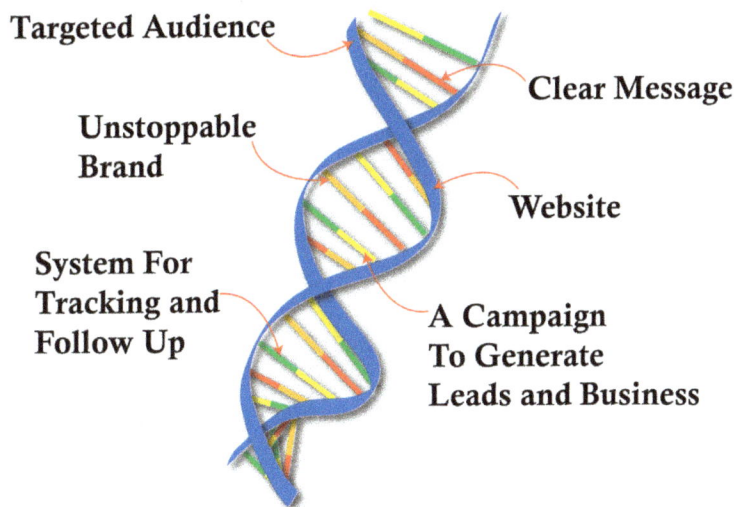

Targeted Audience

Clear Message

Unstoppable Brand

Website

System For Tracking and Follow Up

A Campaign To Generate Leads and Business

What Sets You Apart?

When business professionals come to me with marketing ideas, they often want to start by copying the exact website of a successful business, like Realtor Kristan Cole (www.KristanCole.com). Sometimes they want to copy every detail, down to the text on the individual buttons! When this happens, I share with them that Kristan's marketing success is due to her adoption of the Interfusion Marketing strategy and the roadmap we developed. She has core elements in place for a solid foundation, but what sets her apart is that she has developed her own blend of marketing (her own genetic code) that makes her unique and successful. It's not just her website!

Everyone is different! You need to have core elements as a foundation for success and then you need to integrate them together in your own way to create your business DNA. For example, a website is a core element but could you use YouTube marketing in your business to generate leads versus your competitor because of your comfort level with video? Could your competitors do more direct mail while you focus on email marketing and still be successful? Of course! That is why this book will help you understand the core elements for your individual success and how to leverage different tactics to bring out the best in your business. There is no such thing as one size fits all.

Whether you are a salesperson running your own business, an attorney, a coach, a financial planner, or a Realtor, it is a key element to mastery.

Right now, ask yourself these questions:

What do I want my business to stand for?

_____

_____

_____

_____

_____

_____

What words should come to mind when people think of my business?

_____

_____

_____

_____

_____

_____

_____

What emotions do I want clients to feel when they use my products or services?

_____

_____

_____

_____

_____

_____

_____

What frustrations, challenges or emotions may be leading them to inquire about using my service or product?

_____

_____

_____

_____

_____

_____

_____

If I could solve three of my customers' biggest challenges, what would those challenges be?

_____

_____

_____

_____

_____

_____

_____

Congratulations! You've just taken the first step to create your Interfusion Marketing Roadmap.

Let Yourself Evolve

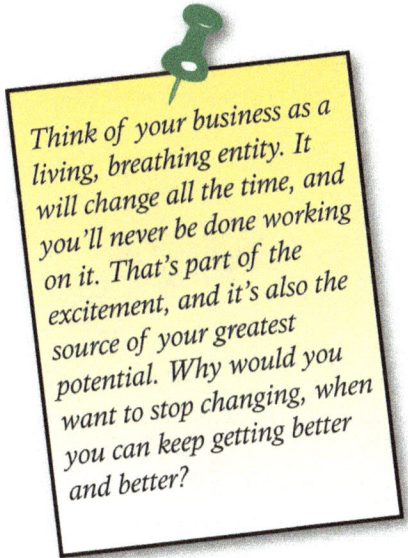

Think of your business as a living, breathing entity. It will change all the time, and you'll never be done working on it. That's part of the excitement, and it's also the source of your greatest potential. Why would you want to stop changing, when you can keep getting better and better?

Where will you be in ten years? You might have a pretty good idea now, but a lot can change in a decade. Your business might have different offices, different customers, different employees—even a different name!

Just as DNA code evolves over generations, adapting to the circumstances to create stronger and smarter beings, your strategy should be able to evolve too. I believe that, in order to be successful, you can't live in the past. You learn from the past, and then you look forward and apply those lessons to what is possible for the future.

Final Thoughts

☑ **Just like DNA has three core elements that build a genetic code, there are core ingredients to your business marketing. These are the essential elements (a plan, a brand, a website, social media and offline presence) that your business should always have.**

☑ **Interfusion Marketing is the practice of blending, weaving and mixing together the core elements to make your own unique DNA code—your formula for success! How much of each element you use, and how you use them together, is up to you. It will determine your results. Period.**

☑ To market effectively, use the Interfusion approach to build a strong strategy composed of the essential core elements. Always stick to your strategy, and always include your core ingredients—otherwise the outcome will fail.

☑ As your business grows and changes, and as new marketing opportunities arise, let your strategy evolve to carry you into the future!

Your Interfusion Marketing Roadmap

Picture the type of business that you would love to have and hold that image in your mind. What sort of people are walking in the door? Why are they seeking you out, and what kind of experience are they having? What does your office look like, and what types of daily activities are you engaged in?

I guarantee you that no matter what your ideal business looks like, it is totally unique because we each have a unique vision or outlook. We all want success, but that looks different to each one of us. Our unique outlook can be traced back to our opinions on three basic concepts:

1. **What do you stand for?**
2. **What's your competitive edge?**
3. **Why does this matter?**

We'll revisit those concepts when we talk about branding, but you should have them in the back of your mind for this section. Here, we're going to briefly look over the Interfusion Marketing Roadmap, a document I create for my clients.

The goal of this book is to help you draw your own roadmap, which will lead you from where you are now to where you want to be.

Don't Follow the Herd

Fire chiefs know that when disaster strikes and people panic, they stop thinking independently and turn into a mindless herd. That herd mentality might help you get through an emergency exit in case of a fire—but it should not be leading your business strategy!

A study conducted by Cell Press was featured in ScienceDaily in January 2009. It showed that it only takes 5% of a crowd to influence the remaining 95%.

This is exactly how individuals get swept up in a crowd mentality. Often, when people have too many options and not enough knowledge of which option is best, they make snap decisions out of fear. That's not how you should approach marketing your business. You want to be strong, confident and knowledgeable about your choices, with a rock-solid strategy in place. Otherwise, you might be inclined to follow the herd without enough thought about where it's taking you!

As I write this, social media is among the hottest marketing tools. Your business probably has a Facebook page—but have you asked yourself *why*? What do you want to get out of it? Are you leveraging LinkedIn? How are you presenting yourself, and with what goal in mind?

The Interfusion Marketing Roadmap is your chance to assess each and every tool at your disposal, including word of mouth promotion, website presence, offline marketing and social media. It will help determine where to focus your efforts and how to craft your own business DNA. As you create your roadmap, you might find that something you've been doing for years is no longer working—or that an activity that's become a rote habit is actually your most effective building block!

To be successful with your web marketing or any marketing for that matter, you need to put thought and strategy into these choices. That will help you move into a leading position, instead of being stuck in the middle of the herd.

This might go against some of the conventional wisdom about marketing, or contradict what your favorite guru says. That's okay. This is about YOUR business, and the key to finding success will be to embrace your own uniqueness!

What's in the Roadmap?

In order to create your unique Interfusion roadmap, you'll start with a good hard look at your business DNA: what it looks like now, and what can be changed to create results.

✓ **Meet The Consumer Behind The Strategy: You'll profile your clients, determine their needs and look at the various ways you serve them.**

✓ **Embrace Your Uniqueness: You'll identify the specific qualities that make your business stand out from the sea of competitors, and learn to use those qualities as advantages!**

✓ **Build Your Brand: You'll learn how to build a consistent brand that attracts the audience you want while building your credibility.**

✓ **Master How To Connect With Your Audience: You'll learn how and why specific approaches work, and choose the tools that will appeal to your customers.**

✓ **Answer Three Key Questions: This is your chance to get crystal clear on the fundamentals of your business, so you can communicate them to the world!**

✓ **Master Extreme Target Marketing: You'll focus in on your ideal customer, and strategize how to serve them the best way possible; they'll come flocking to your business.**

✓ **Build Your Marketing Genetic Code: Finally, you'll put it all together in a cohesive strategy to take your business from Point A to Point B.**

Determining Your Business DNA

Your Interfusion Marketing Roadmap is like **Nitrogen**.

This is an essential element upon which you will build your business DNA. Its structure will give you the strong foundation you need to grow your business.

Case Study:

A few years ago, I worked with Kristan Cole, leader of the Kristan Cole Team and now Vice President for Keller Williams International, to turn her web marketing around with an Interfusion Marketing Roadmap. Kristan is a Keller Williams Realtor with offices in Wasilla and Anchorage Alaska. Their company brings over 40 years of combined experience and a team that consistently leads her local market in sales.

I remember meeting Kristan right after she spoke at a business conference in New York. She was standing beside my company booth and I said to her, "I really enjoyed your talk today." We talked on a personal level and then I said, "Let me know if you ever want some help with your web marketing strategy. I can help you look at all the pieces and leverage what you are doing online."

When I got back to North Carolina I remember one night having a dream about her. I woke up the next morning and told my husband Kurt, "It is so weird. I just had a dream about Kristan Cole. You know the Realtor that spoke in New York." That prompted me to give her a call and later that night she called me back.

I remember the words she said to me that evening. "Tricia, I have had your notes on my desk for the last three weeks thinking about how we can work together and I just don't know where to start in the process."

I said, "I tell you what, let's take it in stages and I will help you every step of the way." So, immediately we began working together. Over the next few weeks we focused on a marketing strategy that would incorporate her business brand, her web presence and her offline marketing with a consistent plan. As we have implemented that plan over the last several years, her company has expanded even further and we are still going strong. We are continually focused on creating cutting edge strategies to keep evolving and moving forward. "Growthward," as Kristan calls it!

We started with an analysis process to evaluate where her business was coming from and whether it was in alignment with her vision for long term positioning within her market. During this evaluation she mailed me lists and examples of all the marketing she was doing including letterhead, postcards, direct mail, client presentation materials and more. She also made a list of all the website products she had purchased in the past and those she was paying for on a continuous basis.

I evaluated every tool she had invested in while she researched what types of transactions her team had closed. We uncovered the fact that 60% of her buyers were first-time homebuyers. However, because of her established credibility, she also had market share in the luxury home market.

Kristan's decades of experience and glowing reputation were bringing her both new buyers and recommendations from experienced homeowners. But there was a big gap: she had little presence in the move-up market, people who were ready to move into bigger homes in the $185,000 to $325,000 range.

"If I can harness that move-up market," Kristan said to me, "We'll never experience a dip in our production again." So we created an Interfusion Marketing strategy that would help her add those buyers to her clientele.

Kristan's team came up with a focused list of neighborhoods that aligned with the first-time homebuyer market, the move-up market and the luxury home market. We then focused on detailed information on those neighborhoods, and talked through each one to determine what made it unique. **Through this process, we came up with the DNA code of Kristan's entire market.**

We created a website with navigation that focused on these markets as well as individual pages to reflect each of those neighborhoods. By doing this, we demonstrated that her company was the best resource in the area for detailed information about her community. Her site provided real facts that people wanted to know as they related to real estate. This helped buyers to know where they might like to live, and what the current market conditions were like. The buyer and seller sections of her site communicated the reasons why those groups would want to work with her team, and why they should hire her.

Within months we were generating high quality leads and ranking on the front page of the search engines. We also had a stroke of luck: the first-time homebuyer tax credit kicked in. Guess who was perfectly positioned with information for first-time homebuyers? Kristan did well by being prepared. Soon after that, tax benefits moved toward the move-up market. She had the information that market needed as well, and she was able to welcome the move-up buyers with great service and an in-depth knowledge of what they were looking for.

That's how you create your own DNA for your business. Instead of just copying somebody else's method or website, get in there and get to know your market.

Learn what makes it tick. Understand the needs of your customers and your clients and tailor your strategy with them in mind. At the same time, look at what makes you unique. Figure out what types of clients you can get along with best, and how you can offer them a great experience.

As a result, Kristan Cole went from having 14% of her closed buyers come from web strategy, to almost 40%.

When you pull it all together, the results will be awesome.

"I was one of those agents who, after 25+ years in business, had lots of Internet/Web presence but none of it coordinated. I had all this "stuff" that didn't work together. Tricia and her team created a roadmap that clearly outlined a strategy to pull it together," Cole said. "The leads I get now are FAR superior to the junk leads I used to get. Also, I am at the top of the search engines and I don't use pay-per-click. I am ecstatic.

It producing effective results. It doesn't get much better than that."

Kristan Cole
Vice President MEGA Agent Expansion KWRI
National Educator, Speaker and Trainer
Keller Williams Realty, Alaska Group
www.KristanCole.com
www.AnchorageRealEstateListings.com
www.WasillaShortSales.com
www.AlaskaHomeSellingInfo.com

Brand awareness and consistency

Specialized information on market areas

Niche market sections

Unique resources

Lead capture

Ebook lead capture

Lead capture

Meet the Consumer Behind the Strategy

I meet many salespeople and business owners that want to create a brand but they don't really know what it is or how to go about it. Coming up with your brand strategy can be a lot of fun. It's your chance to create a unique identity—logo, tagline, website, pamphlets and communications—that really represents your ideals and abilities. But you must always be cognizant of one thing:

Before you can build a brand you first need to know your audience. Understand who you want to connect with and what makes them tick. What compels them to take action?

Many business owners assume that they are their own target market and that their customers will think and act just like they do. But actually, it's pretty rare that you'd be focusing exclusively on someone just like yourself. In fact, your business is to make clients feel confident and well taken care even if they are different than you. So when you're developing your marketing, don't just think about those who are like you!

One of the core elements of any marketing strategy is a deep understanding, not just of yourself, but of your target market and where you want to specialize. In the next section, you'll gain that understanding and create a vertical strategy based on the people you want to attract.

Who are those people? You don't know them personally yet, but with market research and consumer profiling, you can reach groups of similar-minded individuals.

For example, my husband and I love to go on family camping trips. It's a way for us to disconnect from our busy lives, get back to nature and have technology-free fun with our son, Jordan. Because of our interest in the outdoors, there are quite a few companies that might want to attract our business.

Let's say an outdoor and recreation supply company was launching a new line of camping gear, and wanted to get the attention of campers like us. The company might start by researching the types of people that enjoy camping, as well as the types of consumers who might not camp but still participate in outdoor activities.

They would then make a plan that would attract our attention and our interest; they would put themselves in our situation to understand our desires. They might advertise on camping websites or outdoor magazines, and place Pay-Per-Click ads where people searching for campsites would find them. If this new camping gear was high quality and rugged, they might further target younger campers or backpackers instead of families with kids.

The power of target marketing is that your name will get in front of the person you want to do business with and who realizes they want to do business with you. If you can make that person aware of you and offer them something that fits their interests, you will engage them!

They would also zero in on the geographical location of their target market and position themselves in front of that consumer.

Before you can zero in on a target market, you've got to know where your audience is located, what their purchasing habits are and how they go about making the decision to buy.

This will determine how and where your brand is presented as well as how to make your brand appealing to that specific audience.

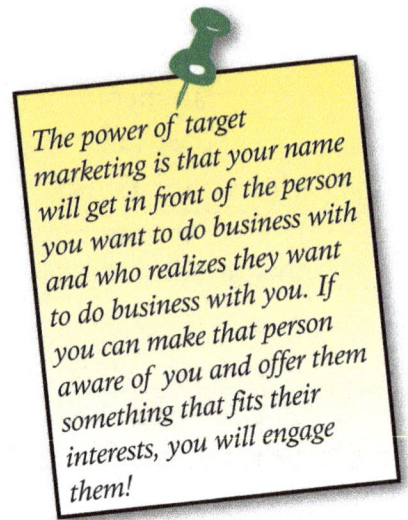

The Biggest Mistake (Most) Business People Make

So many business owners start developing their brand before they know their customer. It's easy to want to start by designing a logo or coming up with a slogan. Most people do this with purpose: "I need branding that relates to my target market!" But how can you know what your target customer will relate to, without knowing who they are? That's a big mistake, and it can cost you everything.

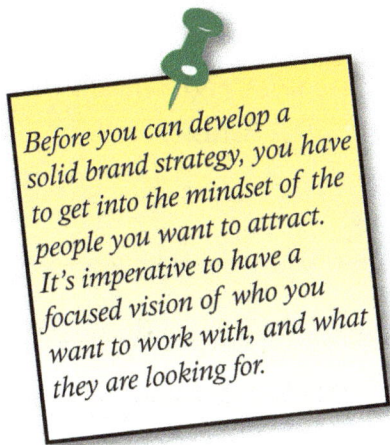

Before you can develop a solid brand strategy, you have to get into the mindset of the people you want to attract. It's imperative to have a focused vision of who you want to work with, and what they are looking for.

As we'll discuss in the next few pages, it's okay—in fact, it's a great idea—to be a little bit exclusive. Rolex is an example. Not everyone buys, owns or even wants a Rolex watch, but the Rolex brand strategists don't worry about that. What they want is to attract high-quality, affluent and classy customers to buy and wear their product. Those customers carry on the brand message just by wearing the brand that stands for prestige, status, and wealth. Other companies like Tiffany's, Mercedes and Lexus also recognize this.

If everyone owned a Rolex, it would lose that exclusivity and differentiation in the market. The brand's identity would disappear, and Rolex would lose the unique statement that people relate to.

There's an important lesson here: If you're not clear about who you're talking to, then you'll be trying to speak to everyone—and end up reaching no one!

Before you start planning your brand, you should ask yourself some serious questions. Working through the questions in this section and the sections ahead, you will become crystal clear on what type of business you want to generate. You'll dig deep into your clientele, and get dialed in to the needs of the buyers and sellers you want to work with every single day. This is the first step toward long-term success!

Meet Your Customers: Profiling Questions

These questions will help you identify three groups of people:

1. **Your existing customer base (the people you're working with right now).**
2. **Your ideal customers (the people you will work with in the future).**
3. **Your evangelists and influencers (the people you've worked with in the past who help bring you ongoing success and connections).**

Daily Bread: Your Existing Customers

These are the people who are walking in the door right now. They are the core of your current business. As you fill out these questions, think about whether you have more than one type of customer. Make a profile for each group.

Where did most of your business come from in the past two years? (e.g. family, networking groups, parents from your child's school, golfing buddies, business partnership, location/frontage of your business).

_____

_____

_____

_____

_____

Describe your average customer in the past six months. What age are they? What phase of life are they in? What kind of job do they have? In what parts of town do they work and where do they want to live?

_____

_____

_____

_____

_____

_____

_____

What do you like most about working with your current customers?

_____

_____

_____

_____

_____

_____

_____

What do you believe to be the biggest value you bring to the table to help them?

_____

_____

_____

_____

_____

_____

_____

Preaching to the Choir:
Your Evangelists and Influencers

Now it's time to look at the people who are out there spreading the word about what you do. They may be satisfied customers, professional contacts, friends and family, even your mom! When you look at them as a group, you'll probably find some similarities. By profiling these influencers, you'll start to see the type of people they relate to. You can also identify ways to continue serving this group, keeping them on as customers and as word-of-mouth marketers.

Who are your influencers? Make a list of names.

_____

_____

_____

_____

_____

_____

_____

If you were to have someone interview them, what would they say about you?

_____

_____

_____

_____

_____

_____

_____

What would you *want* them to say about you?

_____

_____

_____

_____

_____

_____

_____

What do they do for fun? Where do they spend their time? Are there opportunities for you to advertise, sponsor, or position yourself related to their activities? (e.g. team events, family activities, photos with Santa)

_____

_____

_____

_____

_____

_____

_____

"Every year I sponsor a Thanksgiving pie giveaway that allows me to reconnect with my sphere as well as open the avenue of new folks to connect with me. It's a way to be strongly positioned in the market and show my unique services."

Linda Hall
Century 21 First Choice
Top 100 Century 21 National
#1 South Carolina and North Georgia
2013 Technology Agent of the Year Award
Real Estate Tribal Group Speaker
www.LindaHall.com
www.YourGuideToHomeSelling.com

What services could you offer that would have value to your influencers?

_____
_____
_____
_____
_____
_____
_____

Your Dream Job: Profiling the Consumers You Want To Attract

Figure out how to attract and serve the customers you really want, and your job will be endlessly entertaining and fun.

Profile ... who do YOU want to work with?

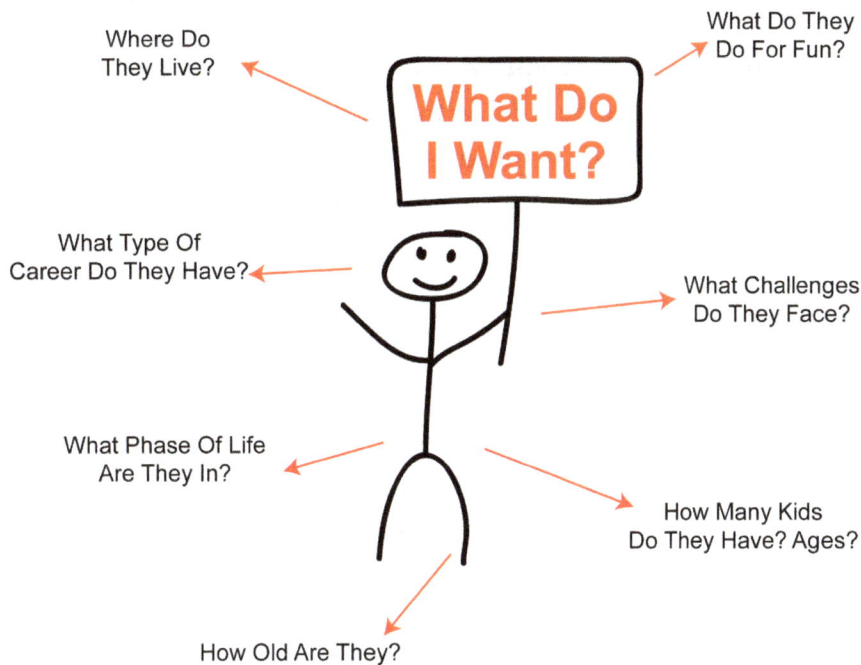

Where Do They Live?

What Do They Do For Fun?

What Do I Want?

What Type Of Career Do They Have?

What Challenges Do They Face?

What Phase Of Life Are They In?

How Many Kids Do They Have? Ages?

How Old Are They?

What are the top three qualities that you would want in an ideal client?

1. _____

2. _____

3. _____

What are the top three "deal breakers" that would make you not want to work with a client?

1. _____

2. _____

3. _____

Profile the ideal customers that you would want to work with every day. Go beyond money and look at the people. What age are they? What phase of life are they in? What do they look like? What do they do? Where do they live? What do they do for fun? How does your business fit into their everyday life?

_____

_____

_____

_____

_____

_____

_____

Now, imagine your ideal client as if he or she is a real person. Invent an identity for them. This is called "profiling," and it's a powerful visualization tool.

Close your eyes and think about that customer sitting across from you, talking about their needs. What are they like?

Name: _____

Location: _____

Occupation: _____

Age: _____ Income: _____

Marital Status: _____ Kids? _____

What is your client's story? What is his/her biggest problem or frustration? What does he/she want or expect as a solution to that problem?

_____
_____
_____
_____
_____
_____
_____

In the next section, you'll turn the focus back to you and what makes you unique. Then, we'll talk about how to connect your uniqueness to your customers, and you'll start to zero in on your ideal target market.

Sample Profile:
Jeff and Donna Honeymeade, in their mid-40s, live in Alpharetta, Georgia. Jeff works as a project manager, and Donna is an elementary school teacher. Their combined income is $125,000 per year. They have two children: Josh (4) and Sophie (9).

Jeff and Donna have been considering setting up a college fund to start preparing for the future. Jeff works for a large software development company, and has recently gotten a promotion that allows him to invest but not sure where to allocate his money. They would like to talk to a financial planner that can lay out the options for the future and have steps to follow.

Determining Your Business DNA

Profiling your clientele is like **Sugar.**

Working with people you enjoy will give you energy, excitement and enthusiasm. That's the fuel that will help you grow your business and have fun doing it!

Embrace Your Uniqueness

Think about a company who got started and everyone thought they were crazy for what they were doing in the marketplace. People would talk behind the scenes and say, "What is up with making desktops in all these weird colors? What do they think they are doing? That isn't going to make it!"

It's a very good thing that Steve Jobs of Apple didn't listen.

So many times we give our dreams short shrift. We sweep our ideals under the rug and try to do what everybody else is doing, believing that it'll bring us success. Well, I'm here to tell you that your unique personality is what makes you stand out from the crowd. So right now, you're going to find out what that personality truly is.

"But I know who I am!" I can hear you saying. Well, that's probably not entirely true. You know who you *think* you are. It can be much harder to figure out how other people see you. Once you do that, you'll really see the special qualities that make you stand out.

The questions in the previous section probably started to shine some light on the subject. You might already be saying to yourself, "Gee, I really think of myself as a business coach, but my customers are telling a different story. They say I am a wonderful resource for helping them decide on a new career. Maybe I should focus on being a career coach." When you start hearing feedback from your clients ask yourself, "Is this in alignment with the niche market that I want to service?" If not, then changes may need to be made to redirect that perception. In the meantime, this also could be an opportunity to build market share in a niche that you are already comfortable with.

Get Real With Yourself

Part of the reason we don't meet our own expectations is that we don't begin with total honesty in respect to ourselves as far as where we are right now and where we want to go. In my coaching and speaking, I've come across many salespeople in the real estate industry who say that they want to work a niche market in their area. For example, they would say, "I want to work the lake market"— but they have never been out on a boat, have never owned a boat, and don't really understand what a lake buyer would crave when looking for that perfect home. They just don't naturally connect to that demographic and lifestyle. Instead, they might be naturally connected to the first time buyer due to their personal experience and age.

I'm not saying you can't work any market you choose. But to have the greatest success, be cognizant of where you are in your business, and where you naturally connect with people.

If you want to work a particular market, you must be able to relate to the mindset of that buyer—and when you work with people that have things in common with you, you'll find that you naturally close more business.

Over the years, your own experiences might shift what is important to you and so might your target market shift. You'll always be revising, refocusing and refreshing your strategy. Just be real with yourself at all times about your everyday life and how you can maximize it in your business.

Work through these questions to uncover your uniqueness.

What geographic market do you service?

_____

_____

_____

_____

_____

_____

_____

How many units/clients did you close in sales volume? What was the median price point of the sales?

_____

_____

_____

_____

_____

_____

_____

Let Your Personality Be Your Guide

Shane T. White is a great example of a business owner who has embraced his uniqueness, letting it enhance and improve his business. As a broker of a RE/MAX franchise in Liberty Hill, Texas he also leads the Shane T. White real estate team. He's a member of Generation X, with two kids currently in school.

Shane is one of those people that you just like from the moment you meet him. He is a calm businessman

Shane has received numerous awards, been a featured speaker at many real estate conferences and is very experienced in running a real estate practice. At the same time he markets his business with a feeling of approachability and warmth that attracts the clients that he enjoys working with.

with a warm personality. He's a person you know you can trust, and a person who shows he genuinely cares about others.

I am sure that if you asked community members in Liberty Hill, Leander, Georgetown or the surrounding Austin area, they would say, "Shane is like me. I have a family with kids, I work and I have a busy life. He gets me and what I need."

"You'll never see me in Dockers and a tie," Shane recently shared at one of my webinars, *"But you will see me in my cowboy boots, jeans and a nice shirt."*

"We are a small community, and we are close knit," Shane says. *"I feel like I'm a part of the community. My kids are in school, so I want to help the schools. Our families love high school football (of course, it's Texas!) so we have family tailgates before the games. I want to give back and share with families and the community while working in real estate."*

Shane T. White
Real Estate Tribal Group Speaker
CRS conference panelist
Broker/Owner
RE/MAX Town & Country
Liberty Hill, Texas
www.ShaneTWhiteTeam.com
www.SellingYourHomeGuide.com

Think about your business. Are you a physician, a financial planner, a business coach or running a professional service business? No matter what industry you are in, if you are looking to build a pipeline of clients you need to embody this core fundamental.

How can you weave your own personality into your strategy? Answer the following questions to start finding out.

What qualities, values and standards define you?

_____
_____
_____
_____
_____
_____
_____

Why do people choose to associate with you? What's in it for them?

_____
_____
_____
_____
_____
_____
_____

When people choose to work with you, what does that say about them?

_____

_____

_____

_____

_____

_____

_____

Final Thoughts

☑ Take an objective and honest look at the things you naturally attract in your business. Capitalize on those things and leverage them to maximum benefit.

☑ Get over the mindset that you need to be generalized to get more business! The opposite is true: The more focused you are, the more credible you'll be. This is how you build your expertise and reputation.

☑ Don't forget about your evangelists and influencers! They are the ones preaching the message about why you are different, and why that makes you the best.

> ## _Determining Your Business DNA_
>
> Embracing your uniqueness is like **Phosphate.**
>
> Your unique personality is the essential element that your entire business is based on. The more you are in your business, the more it will grow into something that makes you proud and happy.

Message and Method

Now that you've identified the *message*—the words and ideas you can use to reach your audience—you need to think about the *method*. As I mentioned earlier in this section, it's more important than ever to work with your customers' habits and their style of researching. For almost every segment of the market, that means solidifying your Internet presence.

A great website does so much more than just prove that you exist. A truly well designed site will provide the ease that your customers want. It will keep them in the driver's seat while they look at information and do their research. It will gently funnel them toward contacting you, creating a solid lead for you or your organization.

It all starts with understanding your audience's desires, concerns and language. Those become your website's navigation elements, information pages and calls to action. As we'll discuss later in the book, these are the same elements you'll incorporate across marketing channels so everything is integrated. Whether its direct mail, online newsletters, social media posts or search engine marketing, it's all about communicating with your audience in their comfort zone, and speaking to them in their language about the things they care about. As long as you do this, and do it consistently, you will not fail to bring in great new business.

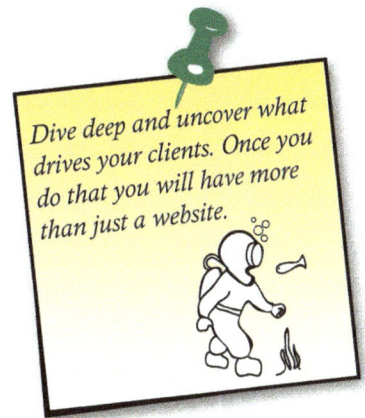

Dive deep and uncover what drives your clients. Once you do that you will have more than just a website.

✓ **You will have a vision.**

✓ **You will have a plan.**

✓ **You will have a strategy.**

In the next few pages, you're going to identify the three key essentials to communicate to your audience. Then you'll do some detailed market research to further identify your specific target market. As you continue to work forward, keep in mind the importance of connecting with people on their level. It'll be important as you develop a standout brand that will truly set your business apart!

Connect With Your Audience

Now more than ever, there is a need to reach consumers with messages that speak directly to their situations, their problems, their challenges and their lifestyle. Consumers have a much clearer idea of what they want more than ever before, so it's best that you speak to them in a very connected way. Just look at the effect of the Internet on the real estate industry. The reality of today's real estate market is that the Internet is the first place home buyers search for their new home, and therefore it is also where they search for their Realtor. In fact, the National Association of Realtors shares in their *2012 Profile of Home Buyers and Sellers,* that 91% of today's buyers— both repeat and first-time buyers—first start their search on the Internet to locate a home.

I'm a "Generation X" consumer myself and I know how people my age go through the process of buying and selling. The Internet is a crucial resource for finding what we want. One of the most important enjoyments in my family's free time is spending time on Lake Norman just north of Charlotte, North Carolina. We spend evenings after work and the weekends going fishing or cruising the lake in our pontoon boat. We load up the boat with snacks and meet up with our friends and their kids. We can't imagine this not being a part of our lives.

We just recently bought a new home. One of the key decision elements was looking for a home that had lake access, boat slips and easy accessibility to the lake. It was our main focus based on the specific needs for the lifestyle we love. In the area where we live, not all homes are located on the lake. So, for us, it was important to find homes by using a map search. Why? We just weren't interested in looking at any house that didn't have easy boating access or have the option for a boat slip. The ability to easily search homes and neighborhoods by map was extremely important as was the ability to see which homes were actively for sale.

You might say, "Well, Tricia, does everyone really want to search like you? You are talking about lake property and that's very specific." But let me ask you something: If you were a lake property specialist who knew the local lake like the back of your hand, and also targeted the neighborhoods I had been looking in, wouldn't you want me to connect with you? Absolutely!

In order to reach your audience, you need to connect with them on their level.

That's why you've spent the time to figure out who they are, and then figure out who you are. By now, you should see the similarities; the common threads that you can use to weave your own life and lifestyle into your sales approach.

Tailor Your Message

Now that you've got the basics, it's time to really dig in to what your audience is looking for. What makes them tick?

Be careful not to assume that every person you want to reach is going to have the same needs.

My family loves being by the lake so we can spend our time together on our boat. But some people might enjoy the serenity, solitude and views looking out over the water instead of having a boat. Or maybe they may want to have a fun place for their extended family to come visit on vacation. Each person has his or her own desires and goals. Your job is to find a thru line of similarity, and then speak to those universal ideals.

The best way to do this is by asking your clients, and keeping track of their answers. You'll also find a lot of information by looking at your competition. You'll get some great insight by reading their materials and their website.

Soon, you'll be able to identify three things about your target:

1. **Their desires.**
2. **Their concerns.**
3. **The language they use.**

Those are the three tools you need to be able to talk to your audience, and once you have them in hand, you can build just about anything!

What are some of the specific things my target clients are looking for when it comes to services that I provide? (real estate example: proximity to schools, price ranges in specific neighborhoods, how to qualify with little money down)

_____

_____

_____

_____

_____

_____

_____

What are some specific things my target clients are worried about? (Real estate example: crime rate, whether the home will appreciate in value, not enough money for a down payment or closing costs, paying too much for the home)

_____

_____

_____

_____

_____

_____

_____

What are some of the words and phrases my competitors and my target clients use to talk about their services?

_____

_____

_____

_____

_____

_____

_____

Interview ten of your influencers/raving fans. Ask them the questions above and write down their answers.

_____

_____

_____

_____

_____

_____

_____

Determining Your Business DNA

Connecting with your audience is like **Phosphate**.

Just as you fertilize your business with *your* unique personality, incorporating an attention to your targets' needs and desires will help it grow and thrive.

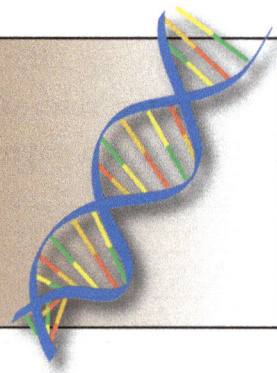

Answer Three Key Questions

Quick! You've got 30 seconds to explain what you do, why it's important and why I should choose you. What are you going to say?

There are a lot of reasons why it's smart to drill down to the very core of your message. For one thing, when that "elevator pitch" situation does come up, and it will, you want to be well prepared. In my coaching and speaking, I use versions of my elevator pitch all the time. I love being prepared and able to explain exactly what I bring to the table; at the drop of a hat.

It goes beyond just pitching, however.

If you cannot quickly cut to the core of what you do, how do you expect your audience to quickly understand it?

A big part of developing your business DNA is to understand those core fundamental elements that make up your identity. Once you have that base understanding, you can easily explain it to anybody who might be interested.

In today's fast-moving world, that's more important than ever before. The whole reason the Internet exists is so that people can get information quickly, easily and on their terms! That's what they expect out of your website. When you truly understand the core elements that make up your business DNA, you can give people exactly what they need, so they'll automatically want to work with you.

The Three Questions You Need to Answer Now

As a Certified Executive Coach, I'm always studying to improve my knowledge, tools and business skills. Recently, at a mastermind event for executive level coaches I had the opportunity to collaborate with Andrew Neitlich, Master Certified Coach and a Harvard MBA graduate who trains coaches like myself to help develop leaders and grow companies.

While working together in a mastermind group with fellow executive coaches I had a huge epiphany. After the session, I realized what a burning passion I have to help people uncover the answers to these three key questions:

1. **What do I stand for?**
2. **What's my competitive edge?**
3. **Why does it matter?**

If you really get these three questions, live by them and practice them, you will be successful in what you do!

It sounds so simple, and yet those three little questions capture everything that's important about your business.

I saw a similar strategy in practice at a business mastery workshop with Anthony Robbins. He had all of us answer the question, "What business are you in?" Of course I said the marketing strategy and business coaching business and most others in the group responded similarly with the category of business they were in. He then pointed out that we don't serve business. We serve people and so no matter what type of business you may have, you are really in the people business. You have to discover what you are really doing. Are you selling homes or are you helping people find a place to enjoy their lives? Understanding this difference is a vital key to understanding what you do and how you should do it. So think about it: What business are you *really* in? It can be tough to find these answers, which is why the questions themselves are an important pillar to the foundation of your business.

1. What Do I Stand For?

In other words: Who are you? Why do you do what you do, and what is the driving force behind your efforts?

This is the question that can have the widest variation in answers. Your motivation can be wildly different from a colleague in your office. It's so important that you always be cognizant of the hidden factors that define your personality. For you it may or may not be about the awards you get. It may be about seeing your client reach their goal. It may be about making your client's dream become a reality. It may be about dedicating yourself to impacting the lives of others.

It's the *motivation* and the *passion* behind your purpose.

When I think to myself, "What do I stand for?" I also phrase it as, "What is the heartbeat, the passion, of what I do every day?" In DNA, one of the key factors is the sugar element—the energy that gives you the rush.

✓ **What gives you energy?**

✓ **What fuels you to strive for more?**

✓ **What gets you up every day even on those days when you are tired but you feel compelled to keep going?**

Some of you may already have a strong mission statement, outlining why you do what you do. Relate this question to your mission statement, but don't just repeat it word for word! Look at yourself in the mirror now and ask yourself:

Does what *I* stand for align with what I want my *business* to stand for?

If not, how can you make them work together?

As an example, here's my answer to this question:

> *"I stand for creativity, education, growth, and innovation. It is my purpose to give hope, inspiration and proven successful business strategies to people so that they can fulfill their dreams."*

Yours might be as different as night and day from mine. For example, you might be most proud and motivated by your 25 years serving families in your community. Or you may be driven by your achievements and stellar sales record. Whatever it is that drives you, use it!

Use creative words and adjectives to describe the emotional part of your business.

What do I stand for?

_____

_____

_____

_____

_____

_____

_____

2. What's My Competitive Edge?

Now it's time to look at what makes you totally original. What skills, talents, ideas and strengths do you have that cannot be easily duplicated by anybody in your field? This will combine your unique personality, as we discussed earlier, and the experience you bring to the table.

What do I provide for my customers better than anyone else?

_____
_____
_____
_____
_____
_____
_____

What's the one greatest thing people stand to gain from working with me?

_____
_____
_____
_____
_____
_____
_____

What experiences have I had personally or professionally that my clients can relate to?

_____

_____

_____

_____

_____

_____

_____

You will probably find that your answer to the first question compliments or aligns with your answer for this last question. Your own unique DNA code is already guiding you in life, and your values will automatically align with your experiences as you get more in touch with your true self.

Before answering the question below, look back at the first section, where you wrote down what your evangelists and influencers say about you.

In the coaching world, we refer to this as doing a "360-degree assessment." You are looking at yourself and your business from every possible angle. What do you see? This is also something that I will do with my coaching clients. We will interview past clients so that we can objectively see the strengths that they bring to the table. It is very insightful.

Are you overlooking the reality of your competitive edge? Or are you putting too much importance on something people might not be all that interested in?

The odds are pretty good that your influencers/evangelists will agree on one or two things that you do very well. If they don't, take the time to think about why or why not.

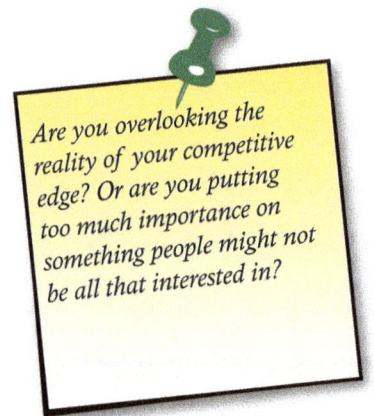

Your competitive edge is your walk-on-water, nobody-but-me quality—the thing you have really worked to achieve.

What's the one thing that you excel at, because you love to do it? Why do people come back to work with you again and again?

As an example, here's my answer to this question:

"I have helped top ranked professionals, many listed in the Wall Street Journal as leaders in their industry, to develop their message and marketing strategies. The proven formula of success allows my clients to create a unique blueprint for their business, and take the guesswork out of implementing it."

Now it's your turn.

What is my competitive edge?

_____

_____

_____

_____

_____

_____

_____

3. Why does it matter?

You can't make a sale without showing your customer what's in it for them—and you can't close a pitch without explaining exactly what people can expect.

"If you don't blow your own horn, someone else will use it as a spittoon."

– Kenneth Blanchard

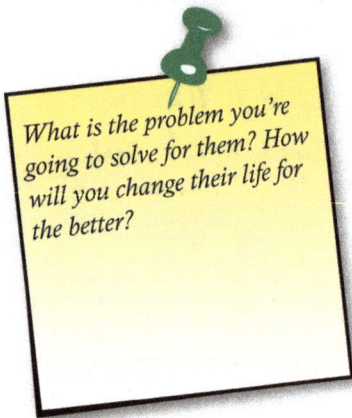

What is the problem you're going to solve for them? How will you change their life for the better?

This is the real, granular, nuts-and-bolts stuff. No fancy promises or big words here. At the same time, you can't sell yourself short. You have something unique and special to offer, so toot your horn!

Put yourself completely in your client's shoes.

For inspiration, you can reference back to where you laid out your clients' top challenges and how you can meet them. Make sure you're also factoring in the work you did in earlier sections, where you delved a little deeper into the desires, concerns and language of your clientele.

Ask yourself this questions and write down your thoughts:

What's that one problem I can definitely solve?

_____

_____

_____

_____

_____

_____

_____

Once again, this is the time to be realistic. Maybe you see an opportunity in your market to work with distressed properties, but you don't have any short sale training or certification. Would it be fair for you to promise sellers that you're the best agent to help them with a short sale? Of course not!

As a business growth strategist and coach, I find that my clients are usually short on time and need to know that everything they do will get them results. I happen to be 100% positive that, if they follow my methods, they'll do more in less time. So here's my answer:

> _"The insights and strategies that I have provided these professionals can shorten the learning curve so they have a clear and defined path of success without having to figure things out through trial and error. I offer a blend of creative and strategy. I can coach, collaborate and innovate with my clients; and teach them how to pull everything together from the inside out."_

What's one goal you can help your customers reach, or one way you can measurably improve their experience? Write it down.

_____

_____

Why does it matter when you choose to work with me?

_____

_____

_____

_____

_____

_____

Final Thoughts

☑ Once you understand the core building blocks of what you stand for, what you excel at and why it matters, you can communicate that with confidence. It will also help your audience connect with you, because you'll be able to tell them clearly and effectively about the things that matter to them.

☑ Interfusion Marketing starts from these basic building blocks weaves them together into your unique DNA. Now that you've defined these core elements, you can look at your business and your clients in a whole new way.

☑ Over time, you and your business will grow and change. The market will change too. Always be ready to adjust, even with these core building blocks, to make sure your DNA is a true representation of who you are and the market you serve.

Determining Your Business DNA

Answering the three big questions is like **Sugar.**

This is what drives your success! It should feel exciting and inspiring. We all have that awesome energy that fuels us to accomplish more. Use it well.

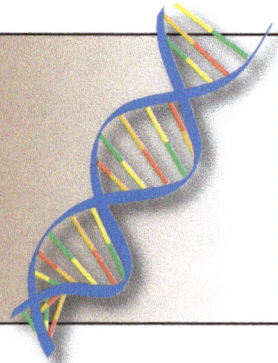

Extreme Target Marketing!

From the very beginning of this book, I've pushed you to really think about what defines you and what defines your customer base. You now have the tools to look objectively at where you are, what you do, and what you want. You probably also have a solid concept of who your current customers are and who you want to reach out to in the future. Now, you're ready to bring it all together with "extreme" target marketing. It's time to identify your unique specialization.

You have already identified your unique core elements, the building blocks of your business DNA. Now, you're going to look very carefully at what you can create with those building blocks. What is your vision and how can you reach it?

You've already started peeling back the layers of your mindset to get at the underlying truth. Instead of working on assumptions, hunches and hearsay, you now have a clear picture of what defines YOU. So now, I want you to start dreaming again.

Think back and ask yourself why you first took a leap into your business. **What was the driving force behind your inspiration to work in the industry you work in now?** What effect did you envision this decision having on your career? This is another "Sugar" element of DNA: the energy that fuels creation and growth. You will use this force to guide and shape what you build, so keep that in mind as you work through this section.

For many of you, **this may be the first time you have thought about having a niche.** Are you stuck in the mindset that you have to serve everybody in order to have a successful business? Finding your natural specialization can result in more sales, happier customers and a greater enjoyment of your work!

Remember, the more you target and focus on the type of person you'll truly work best with, the stronger your brand will be and the better you'll be able to relate to that person.

Take your time working through this section. Do your research, journal your thoughts and ideas, talk to your friends and colleagues, and find your way to your own, unique specialization!

What's the driving force that gets you excited to go to work in the morning? What do you love about your work?

_____
_____
_____
_____
_____
_____
_____

When you picture your ideal practice, what does it look like?

_____
_____
_____
_____
_____
_____
_____

How does this match up with what you already know about your current clients?

_____

_____

_____

_____

_____

_____

Assess Your Geographic Target Market

With your dream in place, it's time to look at the market forces surrounding you, and become truly cognizant of the realities you're working with.

This is a key part of evaluating where you want to focus your efforts in working with customers and clients from specific niche or geographic markets.

What towns do you actively work in or service?

_____

_____

_____

_____

_____

_____

Which market areas (towns) are the biggest priorities? (e.g. where you live; where your office is located; where you want to get more market share) Order them according to importance from 1 to 5.

1. _____

2. _____

3. _____

4. _____

5. _____

Which demographic niche(s) are the biggest priorities? (financial planning example: young families just starting out; clients with young children planning for college, baby boomers planning for retirement, seniors protecting their investments, etc) Order them according to importance from 1 to 5.

1. _____

2. _____

3. _____

4. _____

5. _____

How many client/units did you close in the geographic market, and what was the median price point?

_____
_____
_____
_____
_____
_____
_____

Break down the clients/units to specific towns (e.g. Smithtown = 12).

_____
_____
_____
_____
_____
_____
_____

What is the average amount of business/sales price that your customers spend with you? How does that compare with what you feel you could have spent?

_____
_____
_____
_____
_____
_____
_____

If you could choose a specific market area (town or neighborhood) to have business coming from, what would it be and why?

_____

_____

_____

_____

_____

_____

_____

If you could choose a specific niche to have business coming from, what would it be and why?

_____

_____

_____

_____

_____

_____

_____

Seek Out New Trends/Emerging Opportunities in the Marketplace

As the market shifts, so does the wave of business that you can capture. Meet Mark Spain of Atlanta, Georgia. His business was purely focused on listing and selling residential homes in the Atlanta Metro real estate market. When home sales started to decline in that market, he analyzed his business.

"I realized that people were having no other option than foreclosure due to the extreme declines in home values," Mark says. *"As I talked to homeowners in the market, I saw that I could provide solutions to homeowners so that they were able to avoid foreclosure and have most, if not all of their mortgage covered."*

Mark Spain
Keller Williams
#2 Worldwide in 2012 out of 80,000 agents
www.MarkSpain.com
www.GreaterAtlantaForeclosureHelp.com
www.AtlantaShortSaleandForeclosureBuys.com

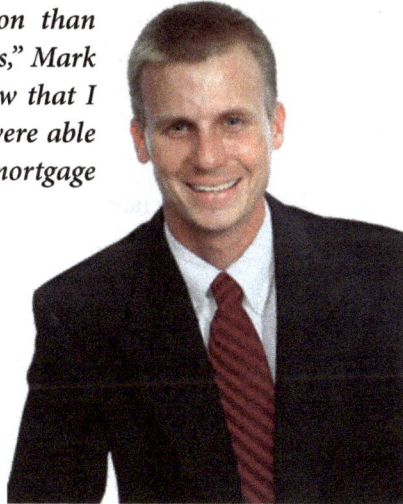

Recognizing this market trend, Mark created a short sale services division to assist homeowners. While other agents were still struggling in the Atlanta market, Mark created a new market and became the #1 choice in that niche. Now, he is able to list short sales as well as residential properties.

Are there new types of clients arising out of something new in your niche? It's possible.

Case Study: Dr. Shapiro of Foot and Ankle Associates

Dr. Shapiro's practice is a great example of this as well. New medical technology has exposed a new market for their practice which allows them to bring in a different niche related patient.

> *"There is a new procedure that we can offer our patients due to the technology that has advanced. There are people who come from all of the state or other states because of this."*

Dr. Shapiro
Partner
Foot and Ankle Associates
www.FootAndAnkleAssociates.com

Hyper-Focus (Develop Your Niche) on Communities and Neighborhoods

What is "Farming" and how does it work?

The purpose of farming is to create a bulls-eye focus on a core area or a specific neighborhood in your marketplace, where you build long-term relationships with clients.

The goal of this strategy is to become the professional in your service/product that people in that area think of automatically.

You want to be the name they want to call.

In the past, in order to farm an area you would have to spend vast amounts of money to do direct mailings and have elaborate marketing materials. Yes, there are businesses out there who do have large farm areas, but this is the end result of a solid strategy.

💡 **The best strategy is to partner your website content with your offline marketing materials and your message.**

This way, you'll leverage your farming so that you build a solid brand with market credibility. You'll create business in a savvy, successful way, with less expense and less effort.

"Our coffee shop is located in the small town of Denver, North Carolina which is a part of the Lake Norman area. People think of Lake Norman first as it is a popular area which is why we want to show that we are one of the premier coffee shops in the Lake Norman area. By having area pages on each main town within Lake Norman this exposes our market to people all over the Lake. They may live in a neighboring town but that doesn't mean that they don't know about us when they come over to this neck of the woods."

JR Hearld
Owner of Cabbellas Coffee Shop
www.CabbellasCoffeeShop.com

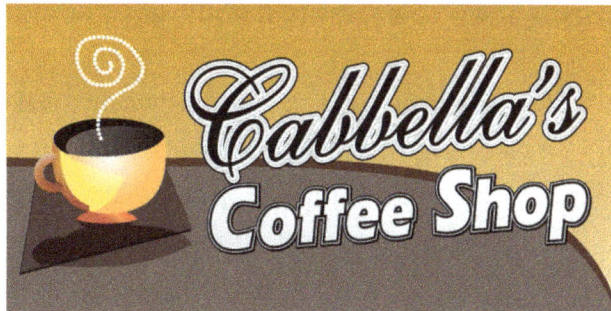

Think about the board game "Risk"

Have you ever played the board game of Risk? There have been many nights in my household playing this game because of my son being obsessed with it! The goal of Risk is to create a concentrated army in strategic locations, so that if your competitor tries to take your territory you can withstand the onslaught. You don't have to control the entire board at first—just be strong in the countries you do control. That way,

if Southern Europe tries to invade Africa, they'll simply be turned away. As your forces grow, you can then start to move into neighboring territories—eventually dominating the board.

In the beginning of the game you have the ability to choose where you want to place your armies. If you try to put an army in too many countries you can't build enough force to roll against your competition. That eliminates the chance to knock them out of that territory. The same thing applies to spreading yourself too thin when it comes to marketing in a large area. No momentum can be built and you will not be able to sustain "the roll" against the competition.

You're not at war with your competitors, and this isn't a simple board game—but strategy is always a necessity if you want to eventually dominate your market.

Take some time to evaluate your market and your farming efforts to get a clear picture of where you should put your focus. Use these questions to research and understand specific areas. You should answer the following questions separately for each area you want to focus on.

How convenient is this market area for you?

_____

_____

_____

_____

_____

_____

Why do you feel that this geographic area or demographic is a good fit?

_____

_____

_____

_____

_____

_____

_____

How many potential customers are in the area?

_____

_____

_____

_____

_____

_____

_____

What are the demographic stats of this market and how does that align to the market you want to go after?

_____

_____

_____

_____

_____

_____

_____

How many children live in this area, and what's the average age of the demographic in this market?

_____

_____

_____

_____

_____

_____

_____

By now, you should be seeing the connections and differences between the markets in your area, and there will be a few standouts that match the outcome you want. Continue working through this process with every niche you serve, and take into account any new trends and shifts. You're well on your way to finding your unique specialization!

Final Thoughts

☑ Take a hard, serious look at who you want to attract and what you are naturally attracting in your business. Capitalize on that and leverage it to the maximum.

☑ Get over the mindset that you have to be generalized to get more business. The more focused you are, the more credible you will be as an expert.

☑ Don't forget about your evangelists and influencers! They are the ones preaching the message about why you are different, and why you are the best.

☑ By taking your offline farming strategy to the web, you will be able to grow your listing inventory, increase market share, and gain buyer leads for a targeted area. This will also show sellers your unique ability to expose their home to potential buyers in their community. We will discuss this in depth in Section 3 of this book.

☑ **Take inventory of your business every year to re-invent, re-focus, and re-strategize.**

☑ **Be strategic on where to focus your energy. The more momentum you have in a specific targeted area, the harder it will be for your competition to take you out in "one roll".**

The practice of Interfusion Marketing is to first develop a kickin' marketing message for the target audience you want to attract, secondly use different marketing channels to get as much exposure as possible for that message. We will discuss how to do this throughout the following sections.

Determining Your Business DNA

Extreme target marketing is like **Nitrogen**.

This in-depth, fact-based planning creates a solid structure on which you can build a thriving business!

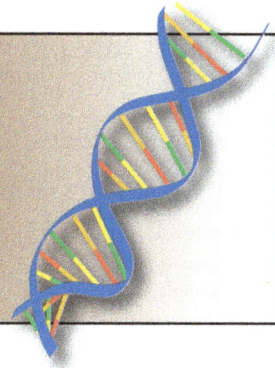

Evolve With Your Market

Way back in 1902, a Minnesota banker founded the Dayton Dry Goods Company to sell quality goods at low price. By 1920, the Dayton Company was a multi-million-dollar business, known throughout Minneapolis for its high-quality merchandise without high price tags. During those years their location was in the city but after World War II they noticed that their consumer market was evolving. People that once lived in the city were now drawn to the suburban lifestyle. They were discovering living in areas well outside the Minneapolis market. As their company strategy continued to evolve they opened a two-level shopping center in Edina Minnesota, a Minneapolis suburb.

That strategy of expanding into suburban markets took hold and now 100 years later, the company is America's second-largest retailer, now known as Target.

Where will you be in ten years? You might have a pretty good idea now, but a lot can change in a decade. Your business might have different offices, different customers, and different employees — even a different name!

Think of your business as a living, breathing entity instead of a product. Just like the relationships with our spouses and our children continue to change and evolve over time so does your business and your career.

That's part of the excitement, and it's also the source of your greatest potential. Why would you want to stop changing, when you can keep getting better and better?

The moment you stop evolving is the moment you start to die.

Just as a DNA code evolves in a rabbit that lives in the beach dunes versus one that lives in the wooded forest, these animals have adapted over time to their circumstances and environment. This is why your strategy should be able to evolve too. I believe that, in order to be successful, you can't live in the past. You learn from the past, and then you look forward at what you can do today and tomorrow. If you are always being mindful of what your market is doing, you will always come out ahead.

Take an aerial view

It is so important that you look objectively at all the factors of your business. In the past few sections, you've really dug in deep, and that has probably shown you new ideas and places where you can grow. The more mindful you are of your business and of the process, the more effectively you can take advantage of new opportunities when they pop up.

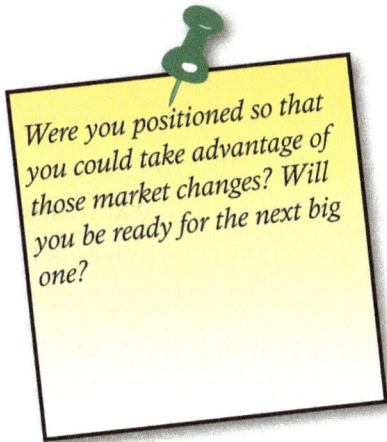

Were you positioned so that you could take advantage of those market changes? Will you be ready for the next big one?

For example: In April of 2008, the United States government announced a first time homebuyer tax credit. You might not have been working with first time homebuyers back then—but if you were able to adjust your strategy to focus on those first time homebuyers, you probably did some good business. The same thing happened a few years later with the move-up and military tax credits. Being able to capture those opportunities can make the difference between success and stagnation.

Evolving with your market can be critical. Once you've got your target market and niche all worked out, it might be tempting to coast for a little while and stop paying attention. But guess what? While you're coasting, your market is shifting in a new direction.

How to evolve with your market

Constantly look at what your market is doing. Ask yourself: "What seems to be moving in my market right now? What are the trends? What do my target customers want? What do my past clients need? What new opportunities are presenting themselves in the market? Is it something that will affect my market or my clients?"

The previous sections have helped you answer those exact questions. Right now, you should know where your customers are and what you can provide for them. As your market changes, just repeat this same process to grow and change with it. Make a goal or commitment to do this every three months.

Once you have that clarity, take it to all areas of your marketing. That is the Interfusion Marketing approach and the key to making it work to your best advantage.

Be mindful of exactly what you're doing and why, and then apply it consistently through a multitude of marketing channels.

When I worked with Kristan Cole to analyze her business, we found that she had a lot of first time homebuyers in her market. So we started working that market, and at the same time creating additional strategies to grow in additional niche markets like the move up market. "Tricia, the first time homebuyers are naturally coming to us so if we build a strategy to reach the move up buyer we will create a long term and very deep pipeline of business," she shared.

By the time the move-up tax credit came out, Kristan had a strong presence in that market. Next, we added a call to action on her website: "Thinking of moving up? Take advantage of the tax credit: click here." We added similar calls to action throughout her marketing materials. Prior to the tax credit, you wouldn't have seen all those calls to action, and you won't see them in Kristan's marketing now that the credit is no longer available. But for the period of time when these credits were a big topic of conversation, Kristan was out there and ready to take advantage of the opportunity.

What opportunity is sitting in front of you, right now, at this moment?

_____

_____

_____

_____

_____

_____

That kind of awareness is exactly what this book is all about. Then you always know you're on point with your message and focus: branding, website navigation, call to action and even where to advertise the message. In upcoming sections of this book, we'll cover each of those areas — but the core of the Interfusion Marketing approach is right here in your real estate DNA and in how you evolve into the future.

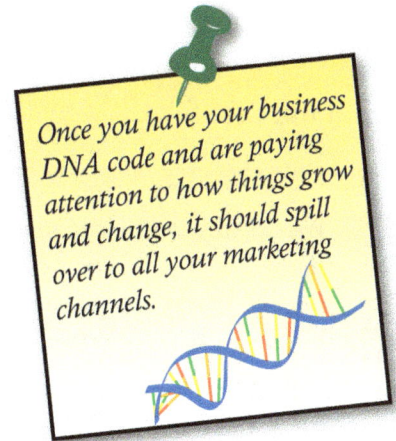

Once you have your business DNA code and are paying attention to how things grow and change, it should spill over to all your marketing channels.

When to stop evolving

Never!

So often, I see people who have great branding and strong market share, but what happens? They get comfortable, they don't evolve, and the market leaves them behind. It's key to understand that you will never be finished growing. Your strategy, and even the DNA behind it, should always be changing as you rediscover yourself and your market. Then you can take advantage as new ideas and channels open up.

The Interfusion Marketing roadmap that you create with this book will perfectly suit your business as it is now, and for some time to come. But don't be shy about coming back in a year or two to reread this book, work through the exercises again, and adjust your strategy! In between now and then, make an appointment with yourself every three months to look at your market and your DNA, so you can be on top of any new changes and trends.

I've designed this book to be as timeless as possible considering the speed at which technology is advancing. The principles you'll find here will hold true into the future, giving you the tools you need to adapt and grow no matter where technology takes you. New ideas bring new opportunities for success, but the Interfusion Marketing approach knows no time limitation. Regardless of the new technology or marketing tools that become available, the strategy will never change because it is an attitude and a mindset for any situation.

> *"We are constantly watching what our customers may want or need. We want to create advertising and marketing campaigns that solve a problem that are in their minds at this moment. It becomes powerfully relevant."*
>
> Purvis Anderson
> Owner of Skeeter Pro
> www.SkeeterPro.com

When was the last time you added something new to your website to address a relevant topic that can affect your business?

_____

_____

_____

_____

What methods do you use to keep up with industry trends that may affect clients?

_____
_____
_____
_____
_____
_____
_____

What further steps could you take to find out what trends and opportunities exist in your market?

_____
_____
_____
_____
_____
_____
_____

If you were up to date on those trends and could relay them in your marketing efforts, how do you see that helping to grow your business?

_____
_____
_____
_____
_____
_____
_____

Final Thoughts

☑ **Always be forward thinking. The moment you stop innovating is the moment your business starts dying!**

☑ **Know your market. Research the data. Dissect it and seek out opportunities to brand yourself as an expert versus other competitors in your market.**

☑ **Schedule a quarterly review to assess what is happening in the market. Ask yourself and your team whether there are tweaks you can make to align with current trends.**

Determining Your Business DNA

Evolving with your market is like **Sugar**.

Trends and opportunities are the fuel that gives your business more power to grow! Stay fresh and relevant, and you can expand in countless new directions.

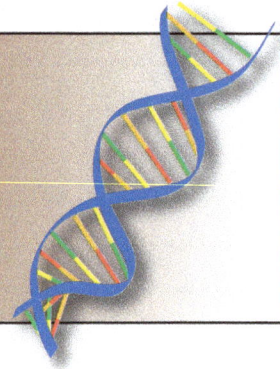

Pull It All Together – Interfusion Worksheet

Building Your Genetic Code

You've done a tremendous amount of work in this first section, and you should already be excited about the possibilities that lie ahead of you. I always say that if you're not excited about the future, you're on the wrong path! At the same time, it's normal to feel nervous. You're making big changes to the way you've always done things, and that can be intimidating at first.

Remember, you are changing your business in order for it to feel more natural for you. It will suit you better, you will enjoy it more and you will be more successful.

There's nothing to be afraid of!

The joy of determining your business DNA is that you gain a really clear picture of who you are, where you're going and how to get there. Though it may be intimidating at first, you'll soon find that it's the most natural thing in the world.

The following pages are your "cheat sheet" that brings together all the concepts and exercises you have worked through in the previous sections. To answer these questions, simply refer back to the exercises you've already done.

Your answers may have changed since you've read through this entire section, but that's okay! Put together all of your ideas and you'll soon see how they fit together to create a true picture of who you really are.

Mark this page so you can return to it again and again!

My Business DNA Code Worksheet

Date: _____

All About Me

What do I stand for?

_____
_____
_____
_____
_____
_____
_____

What's my competitive edge?

_____
_____
_____
_____
_____
_____
_____

Why does this matter?

_____
_____
_____
_____
_____
_____
_____

My evangelists/influencers would describe me as:

_____
_____
_____
_____
_____
_____
_____

People choose to work with me because:

_____
_____
_____
_____
_____
_____
_____

The thing I love most about this job is:

_____
_____
_____
_____
_____
_____

My Customers

I would describe my current clients as:

_____
_____
_____
_____
_____
_____

I would describe my target clients as:

_____
_____
_____
_____
_____
_____

The top three problems that I solve for my clients are:

_____

_____

_____

_____

_____

_____

_____

My Target Market

The geographic markets or specialty markets where I preform best are:

_____

_____

_____

_____

_____

_____

_____

The specialty(ies) where I would like to dominate the market are:

_____

_____

_____

_____

_____

_____

_____

Some new trends and emerging opportunities that I could break into are:

_____
_____
_____
_____
_____
_____
_____

My Goals

How does my current business and clientele match up with the business and clientele I would like to have in five years? Why or why not?

_____
_____
_____
_____
_____
_____
_____

Some things I like about my business and do not want to change are:

_____
_____
_____
_____
_____
_____
_____

Some things I can change or improve are:

_____

_____

_____

_____

_____

_____

_____

SECTION II

Hit the Branding Bulls-Eye

Creating an Unstoppable Brand

A few years ago, when my son Jordan was just in kindergarten, we were playing with sidewalk chalk together. I drew a heart on the cement and asked, "What does that symbol mean to you?" He said, "That means love."

Visual symbols like the heart are so powerful. People relate to those visual elements in an emotional way. Just like the heart represents love, your brand is what people "feel" and relate to your services. It's the heartbeat of your business.

Branding: It's Not What You Think It Is

When you think of the Target chain of stores, do you think of the big red bulls-eye? Probably! But when you think of the actual reason that people shop at Target, you probably think about its affordable prices for quality merchandise, and the convenience of having everything under one roof. Target's logo alone could not possibly express all of that. So how do you know what to expect at its stores? It is because the company has a strong brand that goes beyond just visual elements like a logo. They have made the leap from a visual representation so that the public connects their mission/values with that red bulls eye. Just look at their red shopping carts (which by the way are made from recyclable products!) and you will see that everything supports their brand story and is cohesive.

So many people come to me and say, "I need a logo." I usually tell them:

"You don't just need a logo. You need a *vision*."

What many people fail to realize is that a logo is just a tiny part of a complete brand. Your brand is not just an image or a font choice. It is your entire system for attracting, connecting with and communicating to your target market. It is how you create a reputation for yourself and an emotional reaction in your customers.

Look at Coca Cola, one of the most successful American brands. Yes, it has a distinctive logo—but there's so much more. **The Coke brand is all about giving you an *emotion*** - "Happiness". If you visit one of their factories in Atlanta, you will experience happiness and can even enjoy the happiness factory theater.

What does that mean for Coca Cola? It means that, when people think of Coke, drink Coke, or share a Coke they are sharing a piece of happiness! If somebody goes to the Coca Cola headquarters and doesn't have fun, they'll feel let down by false promises. They'll probably tell friends and family about their bad experience, and that will damage Coca Cola's brand. Throughout the years their brand story continues to connect to us so much it has become a part of our memories and our lives. I remember playing with my friend Karen in first grade. We would sneak into the garage where the glass Coke bottles were. We would pop the top and go in the backyard behind a tree and share it. It was the best thing ever! Now that is my memory of happiness and connection.

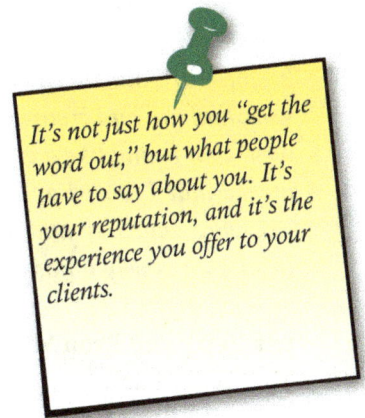

It's not just how you "get the word out," but what people have to say about you. It's your reputation, and it's the experience you offer to your clients.

There is a saying that "perception is reality." How you are perceived in your marketplace will determine people's thoughts and actions around your business. Are you happy with how you are being perceived?

"Our personal brand is probably the one thing that is most responsible for our success. It's to the point that, I have lived in this community all of my life and people I have known for many many years, when they see me instead of saying "Hi Jeff" they go "Hi Young Team". That's how connected we are to our brand. I could argue that Terry and I live our brand but the only reason I can say that is because the brand that you created for us is us. If the brand was not a good fit it would not be natural. It would be a struggle to actually live and be identified with the brand. But because of your ability to sense who and what we were and are and create the brand that reflects that I wear that brand like a custom suit. It feels so natural on me that I don't have to think about it. My daily existence matches and fits with that brand and I think that is why it has been so powerful."

Jeff, Terry and Ryan Young
The Young Team
Keller Williams Realty Greater Cleveland
Cleveland, OH
www.YoungTeamRealtors.com

YOUNG TEAM
R E A L T O R S
FOR THE *Love* OF REAL ESTATE

Five Myths about Brands

The terms "brand" and "branding" are some of the most overhyped and misused words in all of marketing. Here are some common myths you've probably heard.

Myth 1: Your brand is your name, logo, tagline, or unique selling proposition.

Actually, your brand only exists in the minds of your prospects and customers. It's that initial image, description or emotion that pops into their head when they hear your name, think about you, or see your marketing materials. It's how they were treated the last time they spoke with you on the phone, or how pleased they were with your service, or how relevant they thought that postcard was that they received in yesterday's mail.

Myth 2: You need a logo to have a brand.

Logos aren't mandatory for successful brands. They're nice to have, but no one is going to choose your service because you have a nice logo. In fact, unless you have an advertising budget or marketing strategy to spend promoting your logo consistently over time, chances are, people won't remember it anyway.

The reason we remember the Nike swoosh or the Coca Cola logo is because of their constant, high profile visibility including billboards, magazines, Internet ads, and television commercials.

And speaking of advertising…

Myth 3: You need to advertise to have a brand.

It's true that before the Internet, large companies primarily built their brands through advertising. Advertising worked back in the 1950s and 60s because it was easy to reach most of America by running commercials on the three main TV networks or in the handful of newspapers and magazines published.

Today, we're bombarded by so many mass media choices vying for our attention that traditional advertising has lost much of its effectiveness. People are exposed to upwards of 3,000 marketing messages a day, so in order to cope, they filter out items they don't feel are relevant to them.

Smart companies realize that the old way of advertising is rarely effective to build their brand anymore, because they no longer control people's access to information about them. Anyone can go onto the Internet and read reviews of products and services by other customers, and not all the customer opinions are positive.

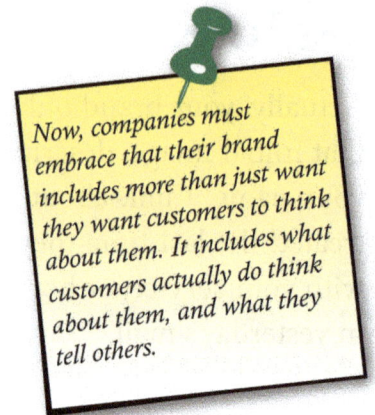

Now, companies must embrace that their brand includes more than just want they want customers to think about them. It includes what customers actually do think about them, and what they tell others.

Myth 4: Once you establish your brand, you're done.

Unfortunately, this is rarely the case. Because your prospects and customers have a say in what your brand is, it is constantly changing in their minds. It is said that every happy customer that does business with you sings your praises to about four people. Every unhappy customer tells between seven and eleven people. In addition to their influence, your core message (heartbeat) may stay consistent but your messages may continue to evolve. Think about Coca Cola in their campaigns over the last 100 years. In the early to mid 1900's the Santa campaign was very popular. Now think about the singing Christmas tree of people in the 1970's television commercial that most of us remember quite clearly even today. More recently the company has advertised on popular shows such as American Idol and is striving to drive consumers to its Facebook page. Even after 100 years, the message is still the same, 'Happiness', but the delivery of that message continues to evolve.

Myth 5: Once you establish your brand, customers will flock to you.

This also usually isn't the case. Your brand may help your company be recognized in your prospects' eyes, but it won't close the sale on its own merits. It is a great tool, but not the only tool in your basket.

For most businesses, your brand is an intangible asset. It is, hopefully, the positive image that pops into your prospect's mind when she thinks about you. Getting people to remember the benefits of your brand is much more difficult and an ongoing, educational process.

Final Thoughts

☑ **Don't just "throw up" a logo. Think about the audience and target market you want to attract. You want them to feel connected to your presentation.**

☑ **Your brand is more than graphics. It's the heartbeat behind your business**

☑ **Your brand can tell a powerful story; why customers would want to work with you and be associated with you.**

Determining Your Business DNA

Developing your brand is like **Phosphate**.

Fertilize your marketing efforts with strong ideas, emotions and inspiration. This process increases your effectiveness by letting your passion shine.

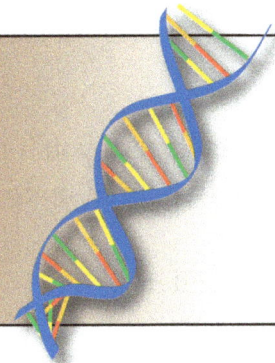

Do the Table Test: Visually Evaluating Your Brand

Most of you reading this book already have at least some marketing in place. In this section, you will take a hard look at your existing marketing, and get all the pieces into alignment so you're truly expressing the power of your brand with everything you release.

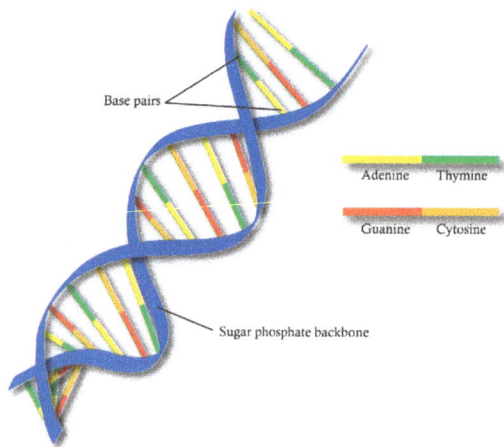

Base pairs

Adenine   Thymine

Guanine   Cytosine

Sugar phosphate backbone

If you don't have marketing materials yet, just skip the questions that don't apply, and answer the rest. Use this section to apply consistency and focus to the marketing campaigns you're planning to create.

Let your emotions run free as you work through these questions. Your passion and your business DNA will be your guides to a brand that truly represents YOU.

The Table Test

For the table test, you'll need a large, empty table and all of the marketing materials that you have used up to this point. That includes:

- Newsletters
- Business cards
- Newspaper ads
- Magazines

- Direct mail postcards
- Website
- Billboard designs
- Vehicle wrap
- Stationery and envelopes
- Presentation materials
- Brochures
- Greeting and holiday cards
- Email signature

Spread out all your materials on your table, and look at them as a group. What do you see?

Check for Consistency

Look at everything: the colors, the fonts, the slogans, the photos, calls to action. Are there certain elements that are consistent across all your materials?

_____
_____
_____
_____
_____
_____
_____

Would you say that you have consistency throughout your marketing? Why or why not?

_____
_____
_____
_____

_____
_____
_____

Are you using an existing logo or theme in branding yourself? If yes, describe it. Is it saved in multiple formats (jpeg, pdf), sizes and resolutions so you can easily use it in new materials? (Note: Ask your graphic designer for Vector Art files and you are covered!)

_____
_____
_____
_____
_____
_____
_____

List the marketing materials that display your logo, and the ones without a logo:

Logo is represented　　　　　**Logo not represented**

_____　　　_____
_____　　　_____
_____　　　_____
_____　　　_____
_____　　　_____
_____　　　_____
_____　　　_____
_____　　　_____
_____　　　_____

List the marketing pieces that have strong brand consistency, and those with less consistency:

Brand consistency is strong	Brand consistency is weak
_____	_____
_____	_____
_____	_____
_____	_____
_____	_____
_____	_____
_____	_____
_____	_____
_____	_____
_____	_____
_____	_____

Which social media outlets do you use to promote yourself? Do they express your brand with a logo or other visual elements?

_____

_____

_____

_____

_____

_____

_____

Refine Your Image

Which marketing pieces most clearly represent you and what you stand for? Why?

_____

_____

_____

_____

_____

_____

_____

If a stranger were to look at your marketing in its current state, how would they most likely describe you?

_____

_____

_____

_____

_____

_____

_____

If one of your competitors looked at your marketing, what might they say about how you market yourself and your products/services?

_____

_____

_____

_____

_____

_____

_____

What are some ways in which you could improve your presentation?

_____
_____
_____
_____
_____
_____
_____

Of the changes listed above, which is your highest priority? Choose the things you use on a daily basis.

_____
_____
_____
_____
_____
_____
_____

Update Your Brand

Whether your brand image is consistent, nonexistent or just a little dusty, it's always a good idea to look for ways you can update and stay ahead of your market.

"Without great branding we are just another REALTOR® out there trying to get business. With a well-known brand we stand out from our competitors and that makes the telephone ring and the computer hum with new clients, referrals and an abundance to fill the pipeline. We have had a consistent brand and now we our team is evolving. One of my key team members is stepping to a partner role so now we are updating the image of the brand slightly to adapt to these changes of growth."

Jeanette Holland - Holland Shepard Group
Realty World First Coast Realty
Beaufort, NC
www.HollandGroupRealEstate.com
www.CarteretCountyHomeSellingGuide.com

Holland Shepard Group

What do you want your brand to say about you? Think back to your core values, what makes you unique and what your clients are looking for.

_____

_____

_____

_____

_____

_____

_____

What concepts should come to mind when someone sees your brand for the first time? Circle your top three, or fill in your own.

Fun	Conservative	Luxury
Spiritual	Hip	Family
Community	Growth	Humor
Wise	Bottom-Line	Generous
Expert	Leader	Trustworthy

Other:

_____

Choose Your Colors

Color psychology is one of the most fascinating parts of building your brand. The colors you choose will elicit a certain type of response. For example:

The color scheme on the left (black and yellow) creates a bright, jarring dynamic, while the scheme on the right (black and blue) is more subdued. Each of these combinations might be appropriate for different situations.

When choosing your brand colors, select a main color that will be dominant, and one or two complementary colors to bring it all together.

Take a look at Skeeter Pro and their website: www.skeeterpro.com. Their main color is a fresh green with white. The accent color is red which catches the eye, setting the tone without using words.

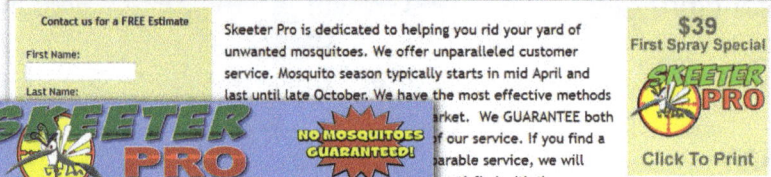

Website

Neighborhood Postcard

Do you tend to use the same colors repeatedly in your marketing? If so, what are the top one to three colors?

_____

_____

_____

_____

_____

_____

_____

Choose two to three colors that match what you want your potential clients to feel when they see your marketing materials.[1]

Blue:
Tranquility, sapphire, dependability, consistency, tradition

Red:
Flame, patriotic, vitality, power, passion, energy, excitement

Purple:
Leadership, respect, wealth, royalty, powerful, passion

Yellow:
Warm, playful, happy, inviting, friendly

Orange:
Strong personality, fun, confident, creative, adventurous, cheerful, thrifty, clean

Green:
Newness, life, growth, energy, health, harmony, serenity

White:
Cleanness, purity

Brown:
Simplicity, comfort, quality

Pink:
Delicate, dainty, romance

Black:
Distinguished, strength, classic, mysterious

Gray:
Classy, corporate

Bright colors:
Whimsical

Muted colors:
Quality, environment, tranquility, luxury

Deep colors:
Sensuous, romance

Look at Your Logo

Why did you create this logo, and what was the mindset behind it?

_____

_____

_____

_____

_____

_____

Does this logo still represent you today?

_____

_____

_____

_____

_____

_____

If not, what would you change and why?

_____

_____

_____

_____

_____

_____

Finesse the Font

This is a critical piece of your brand and an easy place to make a mistake. Maybe you created a new marketing piece for a specific campaign, and picked out a font that looked great for that situation. Bad idea! By using a variety of different fonts across different elements of your marketing, you dilute your brand. Your look and feel become piecemeal and you lose consistency.

It's important to stick with a few core fonts, and to make sure they match your market. You wouldn't use Comic Sans to attract luxury buyers, right?

When I work with clients on brand strategy, we try out a wide range of fonts in order to find one that will appeal to your target market, as well as the people you work with every day. Here's a font chart my company created for Holli McCray.

Below, circle three to five fonts that you like, and that you think your customers will respond to.

1. Holli McCray
2. Holli McCray
3. Holli McCray
4. **Holli McCray**
5. Holli McCray
6. Holli McCray
7. Holli McCray
8. Holli McCray
9. **Holli McCray**
10. Holli McCray
11. **Holli McCray**
12. Holli McCray
13. Holli McCray
14. **Holli McCray**
15. Holli McCray
16. Holli McCray
17. Holli McCray
18. Holli McCray
19. Holli McCray
20. Holli McCray

21. Holli McCray
20. Holli McCray
23. Holli McCray
24. Holli McCray
25. **Holli McCray**
26. Holli McCray
27. Holli McCray
27. Holli McCray
28. Holli McCray
29. Holli McCray
30. Holli McCray
31. Holli McCray
32. Holli McCray
33. HOLLI MCCRAY
34. Holli McCray
35. Holli McCray
36. Holli McCray
37. Holli McCray
38. Holli McCray
39. **Holli McCray**
40. Holli McCray

Logo Fonts

41. Holli McCray
42. Holli McCray
43. Holli McCray
44. Holli McCray
45. Holli McCray
46. Holli McCray
47. Holli McCray
48. Holli McCray
49. HOLLI McCRAY
50. Holli McCray
51. Holli McCray
52. HOLLI McCRAY
53. **Holli McCray**
54. Holli McCray
55. Holli McCray
56. Holli McCray
57. Holli McCray
58. **Holli McCray**
59. Holli McCray
60. Holli McCray

Is there a specific font or font style that you use repeatedly in your marketing? If so, what font is it?

_____

_____

_____

_____

_____

_____

_____

What does this font choice say about you?

_____

_____

_____

_____

_____

_____

_____

Would you consider changing the font? If yes, what would you want it to say about you?

_____

_____

_____

_____

_____

_____

_____

Additional Brand Elements

Now you've got your vision, the next step is to transition that vision into a true brand. It's like putting together a jigsaw puzzle: First you've got to identify each of the pieces, and then put them together until you find a workable combination.

Not all the puzzle pieces will be visual. Some of them tell your story in a different way. You might come up with your own ideas for brand elements; here are three popular concepts.

Tagline

This is a single phrase or sentence that represents your business. It should be very short and distill your brand down to its most basic essence: What makes you unique. You have already mapped out your business DNA. Now, turn it into your unique tagline.

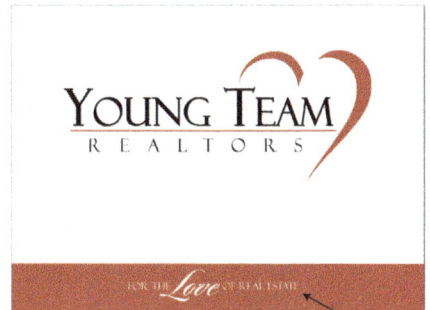

Tagline

"It started out when Terry was an individual agent. One of the things that I admired about her as a real estate professional, compared to many of the other agents I knew, was she always, always put the client first. It was never about the commission. It was never about the deal. It was about the client and their needs. And she basically had this genuine love of serving clients and in the capacity of real estate. And to that end, and she is a naturally smiley person and she likes people. People gravitate to her. So, the heart just became a natural symbol of all of that. The tag line of "For The Love Of Real Estate" really represents how we feel about our work and our clients."

Jeff Young
The Young Team
Keller Williams Realty Greater Cleveland
Cleveland, OH
www.YoungTeamRealtors.com

Explain what makes you unique in as few words as possible. Think back to your earlier work on embracing your uniqueness.

_____
_____
_____
_____
_____
_____
_____

What emotion comes to mind when you solve a problem for your clients/ customers?

_____

_____

_____

_____

_____

_____

_____

What emotion do you want them to feel?

_____

_____

_____

_____

_____

_____

How can that uniqueness benefit your ideal customer? Write down a single phrase or sentence that expresses what you offer to your target market.

_____

_____

_____

_____

_____

_____

_____

Write down two to three possible versions of your new tagline or slogan. Then circle your favorite.

_____

_____

_____

_____

_____

_____

Personal Photo

Not everybody uses their personal photo as part of their branding. If you have a company, for example, then you may want to brand the company as a whole instead of featuring one main person.

On the other hand, you may want to be recognized in your market as a local community figure (think of the mayor, who everybody knows!). If that's the case, it will be important for you to feature your photograph as a prominent brand element. That doesn't mean you need to incorporate it into your logo! It means that your photo is one of the puzzle pieces you can use as appropriate to create your marketing materials.

Whether or not you choose to have an individual photo, remember that your business' unique personality should be the core of your message. Featuring smiling faces can help make that personality stand out.

If you run a professional service business, personal branding will develop you as the expert in your niche.

Symbol or Design Element

Linda Hall (www.LindaHall.com) chose to incorporate star symbols into her branding. Her mission is to provide five star service, and her tagline is "Experience the Difference in Real Estate Service." Her quality service awards and response from clients align with that statement. Instead of using the clichéd phrase "five star," Linda is subliminally communicating her message with this visual element. The stars tell the story, and show clients why it's in their best interest to work with her.

Kristan Cole (www.KristanCole.com), on the other hand, uses a gorgeous photo showcasing the natural beauty of her market area of Wasilla, Alaska. The snow-covered mountains are an element that her clients identify with, and they can be found throughout her marketing. This photograph is a main part of the brand. You'll see it featured from her website to her Twitter skin, her email stationery and her offline marketing pieces.

Picking a graphical element like this offers you new ways to be creatively consistent, maintaining your identity without doing the same things repeatedly. This gives you the freedom to design new materials, without losing sight of what your brand says about you.

Putting Your Brand On "Steroids":

Think how you can carry your brand to other marketing opportunities. Here are some creative examples below:

Hummer

Billboard

Vehicle

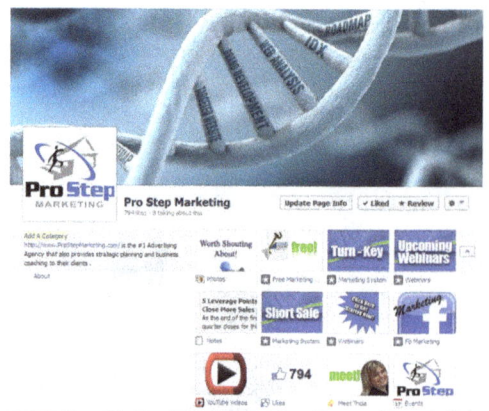

Facebook Page

Personal Brochure

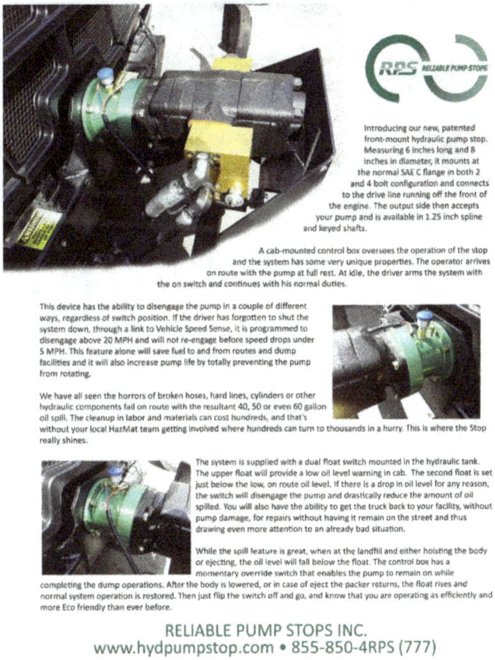

Brochure

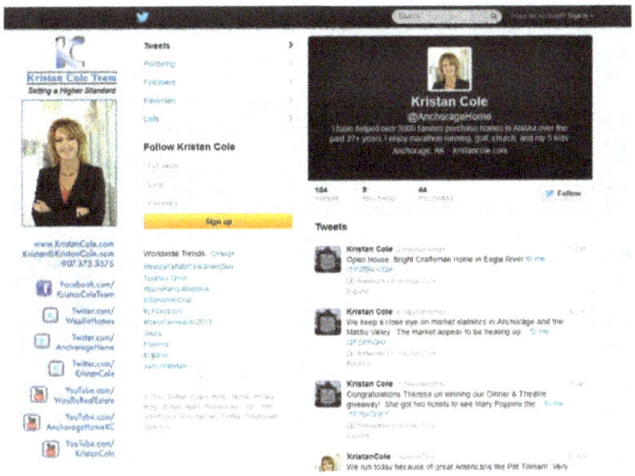

Twitter Skin

Billboard

Facebook Page

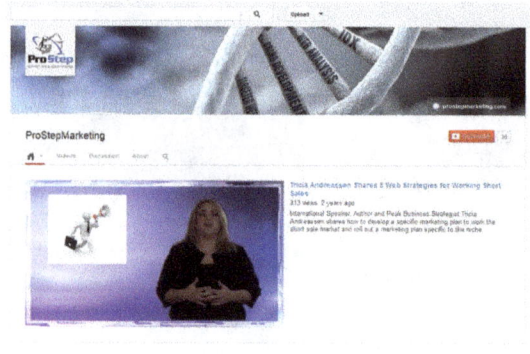

YouTube Channel

Final Thoughts

☑ Branding is the process of connecting strategy with good creativity.

☑ Your brand is the visual representation that PROVES the questions of "What do I stand for?" "What's my competitive edge?" and "Why does it matter?"

☑ Your logo is only one element of your brand. It's just one piece of the puzzle—other elements will blend together to make up the brand. The blend of colors, font, photos and graphical elements along with the message pulls it all together.

☑ Do a table test *at least* once per year. Re-evaluate what has worked and what has not. Be mindful of deviations that might have been made in the presentation of your marketing campaigns that could hurt your brand reputation.

- ☑ Consistency in all areas of your marketing channels demonstrates your professionalism, presentation and positioning. The whole is truly greater than the sum of its parts!

- ☑ Live your brand. Bring your brand to life in all your marketing channels, especially your website. Have elements of your brand dispersed throughout your website to convey the sense of the brand. This can be done through compelling copy, icon elements, and animation.

- ☑ Refresh your marketing materials. Your brochures may have great information, but your brand needs to be streamlined into these pieces.

- ☑ Consistency in all areas of your marketing channels shows your presentation and positioning. Your postcards, business cards, brochures, and email stationery need to portray your brand absolutely.

- ☑ Carry your brand to social media like your YouTube channel, Twitter layout and even your Facebook marketing. Social media can be a huge player in your brand building strategy.

- ☑ Communicate with clients using branded email stationery, email follow-up campaigns and email newsletters. This is many times the very first impression they see of you! You send out personal messages every day. Let your brand come through with your email communication which also provides traffic to your website.

Determining Your Business DNA

Creating your brand is like **Nitrogen**.

Combine your brand elements into different combinations to create a consistent but unique message. Use this brand every day to define your uniqueness and set yourself apart in your market.

Pulling It All Together
– Interfusion Worksheet

Solidify Your Brand Identity

Solidify Your Brand Identity Worksheet

It's time to create the single, unified identity that will represent you, introduce you to your target market and create new levels of success. Are you excited?

What are three adjectives that describe my business?

1. _____

2. _____

3. _____

What is the unique service or experience I offer?

_____
_____
_____
_____
_____
_____
_____

What are my target clients looking for?

_____
_____
_____
_____
_____
_____
_____

What is my tagline?

_____
_____
_____
_____
_____
_____
_____

What colors will be used in my marketing materials, website, etc.?

1. _____

2. _____

3. _____

What will the font and logo say about my business?

_____
_____
_____
_____
_____
_____
_____

What other visual elements (personal photo, symbol ,etc.) will be used in the marketing materials?

_____
_____
_____
_____
_____
_____
_____

SECTION III

Website Navigation

Building a Lead Generating Web Strategy

What's the number one way people research information? That's right, on the Internet. The majority of your potential customers want to find out as much as they can from their phones and computers before they get in touch with a professional. Is that a roadblock or an opportunity? It depends on how you handle it. In this section, you're going to create a strong, effective web strategy to turn surfers into clients by helping them achieve their goals.

So much has changed drastically over the last twenty years and it will continue to change. In the past, you might have gone to a neighbor and asked for a recommendation or possibly used the phone book to find a provider. Websites were at one time considered an advanced tool, serving as online brochures, showing your customers and clients that you were online. But now clients and customers are doing some serious searching for their own to solve problems on their own terms.

Last year we bought a new home. When originally looking at homes we wanted to have a pool in the backyard but, as it turned out, the home we bought didn't have that feature so after a few months we started thinking about a new patio and pool. In the "old" days we would have gone to the yellow pages and would have asked a neighbor for a referral but instead, we used a variety of tools to start our research into the possibilities.

I remember the night we were sitting on our deck overlooking the backyard and saying to Kurt, "How awesome would it be to have a pool to jump into after a long workday?" Before I knew it he grabbed the tablet and said, "Let's see what we can find out." Within seconds we were on websites of pool companies that serviced our immediate market. One of the websites we were on said, "Access our before and after photo gallery with prices – register here now." We were way too curious to pass that up so before we knew it they had received our information. We were a lead. Unfortunately, if you were to ask me what company that was today, I couldn't tell you. Why? Because although they did capture us as a lead, they missed a key fundamental in making a sale. They called us twice and left us a message but they never **followed up** going forward by phone or email. Ten months later we started the process with a landscaper that we chose based on the relationship we created with the person that had kept in touch with us.

Just like myself, when buyers are ready to get serious, they will reach out and ask for more information.

Your goal is to be positioned effectively when they are ready to take that next step. You must PROVE that you are the expert, so that it will be logical for them to want to work with you.

These days, your website must become more than an online brochure: It is a method for you to communicate with your future customers before you even meet them. It allows you to say, "I am the expert you want to work with." But you still must follow up and ensure that promise is fulfilled.

"I think it is twenty times bigger than it was when we started. When we began, there were very few people who really had a living website. Today there are thousands and thousands of Realtor websites. I believe that it definitely feels like a maze for a real estate professional to try and put a website together."

Linda Hall
Century 21 First Choice
www.LindaHall.com
www.YourGuideToHomeSelling.com

Making the Sale: Logic vs. Emotion

We love our home today and it is one of our most treasured assets. In 2006, we sold our home for top dollar, and decided to move into our small rental property for a few short months to prepare for buying our dream home. As the year progressed we became increasingly aware of the housing market struggles arising in different areas of the country. I still think back to the day when my husband said, "Honey, we shouldn't buy right now. We need to sit tight and wait until the time is better for our situation."

Personally, I was devastated: I had picked out the house and the land, and was already emotionally invested in the dream. But I also knew that Kurt was right. We had to be mindful of what was transpiring with the economy. So we stayed in the rental property we already owned. Our short-term living arrangement turned into our home, where we lived through the fall of 2012. We still talked about buying a new house and moving out of our small rental property, but I was not getting my hopes up.

One night in late summer of 2012, Kurt and I took our son Jordan to the local ice cream shop. While we waited in line, I glanced at the corkboard that featured local advertising and saw a flyer advertising a house for sale. I said in a half serious manner, "Kurt, look at this house. The mortgage would be so low."

My casual comment had triggered an a-ha moment for my husband. In that moment, the emotional desire to buy a home was partnered with the logical decision that it was a sound time and investment to do so.

"Really?" he replied.

I said, "Sure. Think about it. The interest rates are so low right now, it's crazy."

That night at home, Kurt sat in the recliner and powered up his laptop. Within

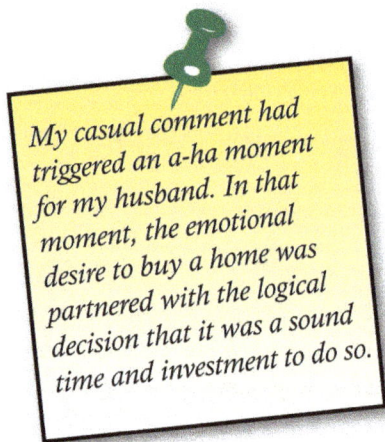

minutes, he said to me, "Look at this house in the Westport neighborhood. Maybe we should go see it." That same night we started running our numbers, and within days we were qualified.

Within six or eight weeks we had bought a home. The best part? It was in our dream neighborhood on the lake, where we had always wanted to live! Something that probably would not have been possible if we hadn't waited.

My story is like many consumers'. In 2012, a study by the National Association of Realtors found that buyers start searching for homes online an average of nine weeks before they even contact a Realtor. Yet, once they contact an agent, it takes them only three weeks to buy.

If you are a real estate agent, so much of the buying process is invisible to you. It's the long conversations your potential customers have about how much $300,000 can buy, how many bedrooms they want, which neighborhoods they want to live in, and what homes are for sale in those neighborhoods. It's the Sunday mornings when they get up and drive around town with a list of homes they found on the Internet, because they were able to do their own research. Like my husband and me, your buyers are doing as much of the preparation as they can on their own terms.

When do buyers get serious? It happens when their passion is ignited and their logic is justified. A great website will facilitate both of those things. For example, you might show beautiful photos of homes in your target market to get people's imaginations working. Or you might include descriptions of various neighborhoods and why they are great places to live. The desire to own a property that suits them and improves their lives—that is what feeds buyers' passion. Meanwhile, you might provide information on the market, or the ability to search homes by specific price ranges and features. That feeds the logical side, demonstrating the viability of making the purchase.

Combine emotions with logic, and your site will engage consumers alike. Strive to have the website that people will visit when they are fired up and ready to make a decision, and help make that decision easy!

In This Section

This section of the book will take you step-by-step through the process of building a standout website that will crush the competition.

1. **The Top Ten Things Your Website Must Have** - You will break down the core, non-negotiable elements of a great website layout.

2. **Own Your Specialization and Niche** – You will learn tactics for proving that you have the expertise in your target market.

3. **Calls to Action, Offers and Educational Marketing** – You will learn to create a sense of urgency or an offer consumers "can't resist."

4. **Lead follow up, management and conversion** – You will learn how to offer real benefits and incentives for joining your mailing list, plus strategies to keep your contacts active and engaged.

5. **Interfusion: Website Navigation Worksheet** – You'll create your website DNA, streamline your ideas and compile your killer strategy.

The Ten Things Your Website Must Have

Did you ever watch *The Muppets*? Remember the mad scientist Dr. Bunsen Honeydew and his assistant Beaker? Poor Beaker was always getting in trouble. I remember watching Dr. Honeydew mix chemicals together to make a formula—but he would make a mistake causing the whole thing to blow up in Beakers face!

It's comedy when puppets and cartoon characters work hard on something only to have it fail spectacularly. But when you spend time and money on something important, you need to know it's going to work. Still, if one component is missing—if you mix the elements incorrectly or add too much of one thing—you can wind up with a disaster on your hands.

Over the years, I have created business roadmaps as well as marketing and web strategies for businesses throughout the world. What I've found is that there are certain non-negotiable elements that your website absolutely must have, in the right combination. If you don't follow the formula, you really won't get the results you want. KABOOM! You'll be sitting there scratching your head and saying, "Why didn't that work? I thought my ideas were great!"

Your ideas are probably pretty good, but this is a tried-and-true science based on strategy and results. This is why we've worked hard to develop the DNA

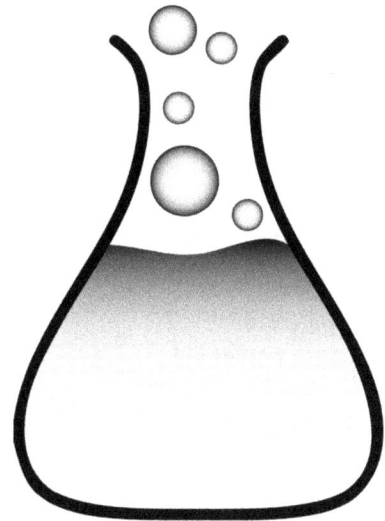

for your business and a strong, detailed brand strategy. Without this kind of in-depth comprehension and mindfulness of what your strategy is, you're just making it up as you go along.

The next step is to incorporate all that planning and strategy into your website framework. Here are the ten non-negotiable, got to-have-it elements for a truly successful site.

#1: Your overall presentation must have a message and a story.

Now that you've worked through the previous sections of this book, you should have a solid brand and a set of specific things that you stand for. Now, your brand needs to come to life on your website. This doesn't just mean updating your homepage with visuals and content that will compel your target customer to click in. It also means updating your entire site so that every page seamlessly represents your brand.

Your fonts, colors, and general "vibe" need to be incorporated into your website, just like your offline marketing. Otherwise, why did you do all that work on your branding just to lose potential business when they click to a competitor's site?

Often I see business professionals who have a great-looking website but when you click through to the articles or more information you wind up on another site or in an area with a completely different look. Even worse, you lose the lead after all the work driving them to you. When that happens, you lose the continuity of your branding. People lose contact with your message, and they connect with something new instead.

Does your website have a message and a story?

☐ Yes, my brand comes to life seamlessly on my website!

☐ No. I want my website to achieve these goals:

_____

_____

_____

_____

_____

_____

_____

#2: You must give people a reason, a compelling need to stay on your site.

In the navigation bar on your website, what do your menu items say? Let me guess—"Home, Our Services, About Us, Contact." Those are the standard navigation items, and they don't say anything about why the person should even check out your site. It doesn't answer the three key questions. It doesn't make you unique. It doesn't _prove_ anything.

You've got to get more personal!

Your site is the proof that you are the expert in the market you service. Your expertise is what makes people want to stay on your site. Show them that you can give them what they are looking for. If you are a financial planner that might be pages on saving for college, nest eggs for retirement, or it might be steps for the newlywed couple on how to get started.

The same thing goes for market trends. What is a relevant topic that is affecting your client base? It's smart to have special information that appeals to that group. For example, if you are in real estate and have lots of first-time homebuyers, offer a free resource and data spreadsheet on the benefits of buying vs. renting and the money comparison. If they see you're experienced with what they need, they will stick around.

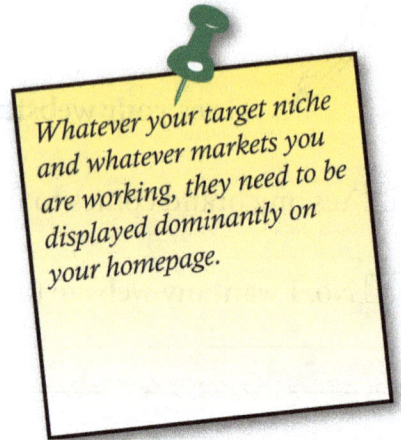

Whatever your target niche and whatever markets you are working, they need to be displayed dominantly on your homepage.

Does your website prove your expertise and give visitors a real reason to stay?

☐ Yes, I have customized website features that really speak to the target market and niche I service, and my website statistics show that it's working!

☐ No. I want my website to achieve these goals:

_____

_____

_____

_____

_____

_____

_____

#3: You must romance the customer and let them feel comfortable.

Clearly, you can't just give out free information, then sit back and wait for the cows to come home. If you want to continue to have a relationship with your website visitors so that they turn into customers at some point, you need to keep in touch with them. That means capturing their email address or phone numbers and streamlining them into a long term follow-up strategy.

However, if you come on too strong you'll just push them away. It's like going on a first date: You want people to feel comfortable about visiting your site. You need to romance them by building up a level of trust and confidence. Show potential customers your experience and your commitment to help them reach their goals, and then when they are invested in the process, ask them to make a commitment to you.

Building a relationship is of the utmost importance.

Does your website prompt registration in certain sections without being pushy and at the same time giving them something of value?

☐ Yes, and I am happy with the number and quality of my website leads!

☐ No. I want my website to achieve these goals:

_____

_____

_____

_____

_____

_____

#4: You must offer useful tools and information in their research process.

Let's say you've got a button that says, "Looking to build a solid retirement portfolio? Click here for the seven step strategy." Where does that link take your visitor? If it goes straight to a form that they need to fill out so you can contact them later, they're probably going to refuse. You haven't offered them anything of value yet. They want to get information on what it would look like for them if they knew the steps and could get started right away. Once they see that it's possible for them to achieve their dreams with you, then you can ask them for contact information.

When you put up a lead-generating element in your site you must make sure that it really gives your visitors what they want. It should be informative and compelling, to make them want more.

Does your website offer information your visitors can really use?

☐ Yes, I have great resources available for each of my target markets.

☐ No. I want my website to achieve these goals:

_____

_____

_____

_____

_____

_____

#5: You must practice the five second rule.

On this list, #2 and #5 go hand-in-hand. Let's say you are in real estate. When you provide information on condos, you should also provide a MLS search that will turn up condominium properties for sale in the specific market they are interested in. What good is a button that says "click here to find out more about condos" when it just turns up a general search full of regular homes they aren't interested in? Rule #2 said you must give clients a compelling reason to stay on your site, but rule #5 highlights the fact that you must offer that information quickly, in an easy to understand way.

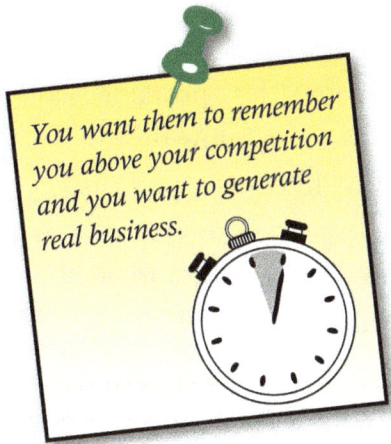

You want them to remember you above your competition and you want to generate real business.

Be mindful that when your visitors click through to a specific page, they are looking for specific information and if you don't deliver, they will expect you not to be able to deliver on anything else.

On the homepage they should be able to find and get to the information they need within those first five seconds. This also applies when they click through to a specific page. Once they are into your site the five second rule should apply on every page.

Does your website provide custom targeted information they can find in less than five seconds with specific results?

☐ Yes, my target visitors can find exactly what they are looking for in a couple of clicks!

☐ No. I want my website to achieve these goals:

_____

_____

_____

_____

_____

_____

#6: You must incorporate lead capture into the process.

Prospective buyers do most of their shopping independently. They probably won't get in touch with you until they find something that they want to know more about. When that happens, you need to make sure they have a way to contact you easily.

What good is it if you spend all the effort to drive people to your website and get them fired up, only to have them leave immediately or go straight to your competitor?

Give your visitors lots of ways to ask you for more information. You might allow them to: Schedule an appointment, ask for more details via email, map your location, and share your site with a friend or on social media. Different types of lead mechanisms will compel different types of people.

Does your website effectively capture leads?

☐ Yes, I get great leads every day from my site!

☐ No. I want my website to achieve these goals:

_____

_____

_____

_____

_____

_____

_____

#7: You must have an automated follow-up campaign behind the lead capture.

Even after your potential customers have registered with you, they might not be ready to take action. Buyers can sometimes wait for years until they are ready. As their decision-making process moves forward, your job is to make sure you're positioned in front of them consistently as the expert. When they are ready to go to the next step you should be top of mind.

Do your website leads receive regular follow-ups and information related to their interests?

☐ Yes, I am effectively keeping in touch with my contacts until the moment they decide to move forward!

☐ No. I want my follow-up relationship campaigns to achieve these goals:

_____

_____

_____

_____

_____

_____

#8: You must have a lead management strategy in place.

Sales are won and lost within minutes. If a visitor fills out your contact form, then goes to a competitor's site and fills out their form, how long do you have before your competitor follows up?

You don't want to be working out in the field when a lead comes in, then have to run back to your office and put the information into your database. That lost time can lose you major business. Instead, your visitor should receive an instant, automated response within minutes.

The more seamlessly you can automate the data getting from your contact form to your email, the stronger you will be. It's important to not only generate the lead but have systems in place to track the process.

Is your database automating lead responses and follow-up?

☐ Yes, I feel confident that every lead funnels into a follow up system and I am able to track their progress!

☐ No. I want my system to achieve these goals:

_____

_____

_____

_____

_____

_____

_____

#9: You must advertise and get the word out across multiple channels.

What good is having a website if nobody sees it? The key to a great website and brand is to generate significant amounts of exposure and traffic. Plan out campaigns, strategies and ideas to get more people viewing your site. Constantly be in promotions phase: At a dinner out, at social events, in your email and all your communications. The list goes on!

Are you constantly driving traffic to your website?

☐ Yes, people love my site and I'm promoting it constantly!

☐ No. I want my promotions to achieve these goals:

_____

_____

_____

_____

_____

_____

#10: You must have unique offers that get them further engaged in the process with you.

Consumers are constantly on the hunt for information that is worth something of value to their particular situation. Use educational marketing to keep them informed and solidify your expert image. Tools like Ebooks, white papers, checklists, calculators and more are imperative to the strategy.

Are you offering Ebooks and checklists to generate interest and capture the lead?

☐ Yes, people constantly register to gain access to my unique tools (not generic ones that came with my website template) and education!

☐ No. I want to add these particular strategies to achieve these goals:

_____

_____

_____

_____

_____

_____

Final Thoughts

☑ **All ten of these elements must work together for you to see maximum results from your website strategy.**

☑ **If one, and only one, is missing you will not get the best results.**

☑ **Don't underestimate the power of blending! The more ways you can reach people, show them you know your market and give them exactly what they need, exactly when they need it—the more completely you will dominate. That's the power of Interfusion Marketing.**

☑ **Think of your website navigation and strategy as living, breathing processes. You will never be finished making changes and improvements, evolving with your market and trying new things. Make sure these ten elements are always at the front of your strategy, even as your website grows and changes.**

Determining Your Business DNA

The non-negotiable website strategy is like **Nitrogen**.

This unchanging formula is the structure that will support your business, no matter how big and successful it gets.

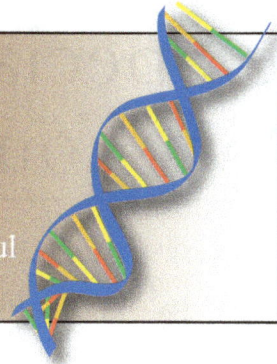

Be Specialized and Own Your Niche

Now that you're truly aware of what sets you apart, what markets you want to work, and who your target market is, it's time to OWN it! To do that, you need to prove that you are the expert. When people see your marketing, your advertising, and your website, they need to immediately understand exactly what you stand for. I call this the five second rule.

When someone visits your website, they should have no doubt that they've come to the right place, and that you are the expert who can help them.

A niche is not a prison. A niche is a focus on where to put your energy, your message, and your marketing. The more clarity in your message and the information you provide, the stronger the engagement will be with the person you want to attract.

Does that sound impossible? It really isn't. If you're being mindful of how all the pieces fit together, you can dominate your niche. And by doing so, you'll be making a smart move for the growth and stability of your business.

The five second rule applies when somebody sees your marketing of any kind — whether it be your website, your direct mail piece, your brochure, or an advertisement, it should grab them and make them want to take action immediately.

Your target market is the consumer/client you serve. Your niche is the service you provide to your target market to solve their problem.

Why Owning Your Niche is a Wise Choice

Think about the major decisions you've made in your life. There aren't very many of them: education, career choice, marriage, kids, home ownership. You can probably list them all in a few seconds, but these are the choices that define your entire life. Did you make them lightly? Of course not! Did you seek out advice and guidance? For most of us, we look to an expert or a qualified resource when our happiness and future are on the line.

As an example: My father-in-law has a serious heart condition. Recently, he needed to receive an advanced procedure. In order to get the very best treatment available, he drove all the way from his home in Michigan to Cleveland, Ohio, so he could see the specialist with the most experience treating his condition. Wouldn't you do the same? If you needed heart surgery, you wouldn't go to a general practitioner or even to a doctor with cardiac experience. You would seek out the specialist who could give you the best treatment, so you could get better as soon as possible and get back to living.

When making big purchasing decisions, customers want to partner with a market expert who has real training and experience—somebody who can help them have the best experience possible and get the best return on their investment.

Being Generic Doesn't Work

There is power in being able to show that you are the expert in your niche. Don't dilute your power by trying to be everything to everyone. Own your specialization, dominate your market, and grow from there.

Case Study: Dr. Shapiro
Dr. Shapiro's practice is in the Lake Norman market of Charlotte, North Carolina. When I sat down with Dr. Shapiro, he said to me: "I always knew I wanted to be a

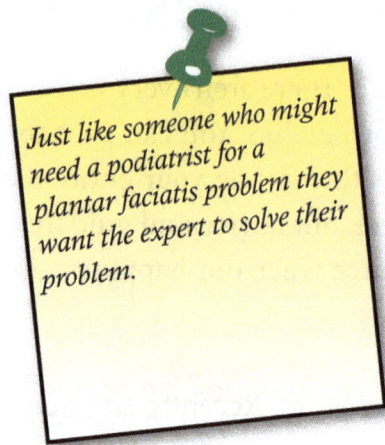

Doctor and my passion grew when I worked with some other Doctors during my premed studies that focused on the foot and ankle. I loved what they were doing and I decided that I wanted to work in this specialty. I think it is very important to specialize. Medicine is so broad these days and the knowledge base is larger than it was 100 years ago. It is hard for a general practitioner to tackle everything."

Just like someone who might need a podiatrist for a plantar faciatis problem they want the expert to solve their problem.

Since his practice focuses helping patients with specific problems related to their foot and ankle, the website is also highly specialized to provide quality information. The result? "Our practice continues to grow. We are highly referred by other physicians, which is very important to us and our clients refer us as well, creating long term relationships," he says.

Take a look at Linda Hall's homepage below showing a navigation button for Fort Mill. When you click the button you land on an interior page dedicated to that area. The Fort Mill page has useful content and video, as well as MLS searches for homes in this specific area.

Search homes for sale

Video of area

Content

"Even though my target market is small, I am currently ranked #1 in South Carolina and North Georgia for Century 21 and ranked #52 nationally. I have tracked over 50% of my closed business coming from my website. Why? Because I focus on my audience. I think about their needs, their problems, and their questions so that I can address them and help them move forward."

Linda Hall
Century 21 First Choice
www.LindaHall.com
www.YourGuideToHomeSelling.com

How To Own Your Niche On Your Website

It's crucial that your website really speaks to the people you want to work with, and gives them exactly what they are looking for. If you accomplish this, your visitors will come back again and again, and eventually choose you as the agent they want to work with—just like they did with Linda Hall.

What are some things you could provide on your website to prove you are the expert?

_____

_____

_____

_____

_____

_____

Website Navigation and Content Pages

As we discussed in the previous section, your navigation needs to have buttons and menu items for the markets or type of client you want to focus on. By creating content pages and navigation elements for your market, you are demonstrating your expertise and providing value for your target clients! You may be a financial planner that exclusively works with baby boomers and seniors instead of the young person just starting out. You may be an executive coach that only focuses on leadership training and not on middle management evaluations.

Think about how you can specialize. Is it working with a particular industry, a specialized niche or a concentrated geographic market? Just by doing this, you'll set yourself apart from the majority of your competition!

Whatever your individual approach, always be sure to visually feature the various niches you want to work actively. This is Interfusion Marketing in action! You know what makes you unique, so be cognizant of that, and leverage it consistently. Know what your audience wants. Know what they desire. Know what keeps them up at night, and give them solutions. If you do this, you will become the real estate expert that your target market chooses above the rest.

Look back to the niche markets you have already identified. Which of them can you start dominating right now?

_____

_____

_____

_____

_____

_____

_____

Which of the niches you identified are the most active, or have the most potential for new business?

_____

_____

_____

_____

_____

_____

_____

What are some ways you can showcase to demonstrate your expertise? Think about the areas you want to focus on, as well as the types of consumer demographics you want to specialize in.

_____

_____

_____

_____

_____

_____

_____

Final Thoughts

☑ **Even though you might think that your website is doing its job, take a look at your website with a fresh approach.**

☑ **Think like a buyer. What would they want when they land on your site? What is the problem that keeps them up at night? What problems do you solve for them?**

☑ **The more you connect emotionally with the consumer the stronger the engagement they will have with you** – *compelling them to want more.*

☑ **A niche is really a focus on where you want to place your energy—whether it be an area of specialty, a demographic or a geographic market.**

☑ **A niche is not a prison. Its purpose is not to limit you. It is meant to make you the only choice, the expert.**

☑ **Prove that you know your niche. Set up your website and your marketing to communicate your specialization and give useful information immediately.**

✓ **Follow the five second rule! Will they see what you can provide them right away?**

✓ **Give your target customers what they want. Solve their problems, and you will have a client for life.**

Determining Your Business DNA

Owning your niche on your website is like **Phosphate**.

By investing your energy and focus in the markets you want to dominate, you create more opportunities, connections and new business in your unique niche.

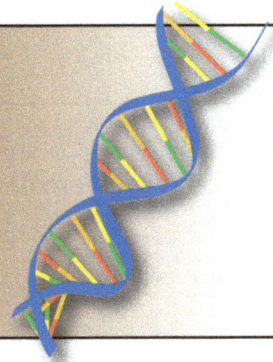

Do a self-test on your website.

Pretend you are one of your target customers. Go through your website and get detailed information just as they would. Could you find what you wanted? How easy is it? What could be better?

_____

_____

_____

_____

_____

_____

_____

Are you getting the lead?

_____
_____
_____
_____
_____
_____
_____

☐ They can easily email me

☐ They are challenged seeing what I provide uniquely from others.

Do the self-test of your search three or four times, pretending each time that you are a different type of target customer. What did you find?

_____
_____
_____
_____
_____
_____
_____

Blending: Calls To Action →
Offers → Lead Capture
(Educational Marketing)

As you start building your website navigation and proving your expertise in your niche, you are creating elements that compel your website visitors to click through and get more information. Now it's time to sprinkle in calls to action.

Calls to action are headlines that capture their attention to get the person thinking differently. Here is an example. Even though I love Lake Norman, one of my favorite places is the coastal area of Georgia. If Kurt and I were looking to buy a second home in St. Simons Island, what would compel me to buy a few years earlier than the plan in my brain? Here's the scoop. I might be thinking about it for ten years from now. Imagine if there was a website I could go to with a button that said, "Find your dream home and build your retirement portfolio, all at the same time. Click here to find out more."

After clicking the button, there would be a white paper/Ebook/checklist on how to plan for the future and possibly move that timeline up from ten years to three years, making my dream a reality.

This is a prime example of getting a person to engage with you because of the "lightbulb" moment going off in their brain. Offer them a new way to look at a situation while combining emotion with logic. You'll show them the possibility of what they may really want in a way they didn't know they could accomplish it.

Give them the idea and plan the scientific formula to get them into an email follow-up campaign.

Why and how to use calls to action

Calls to action are important because they get people thinking in a different way. Once you have a prospect's attention, you offer something of value, and in exchange you can ask for something, like their email address.

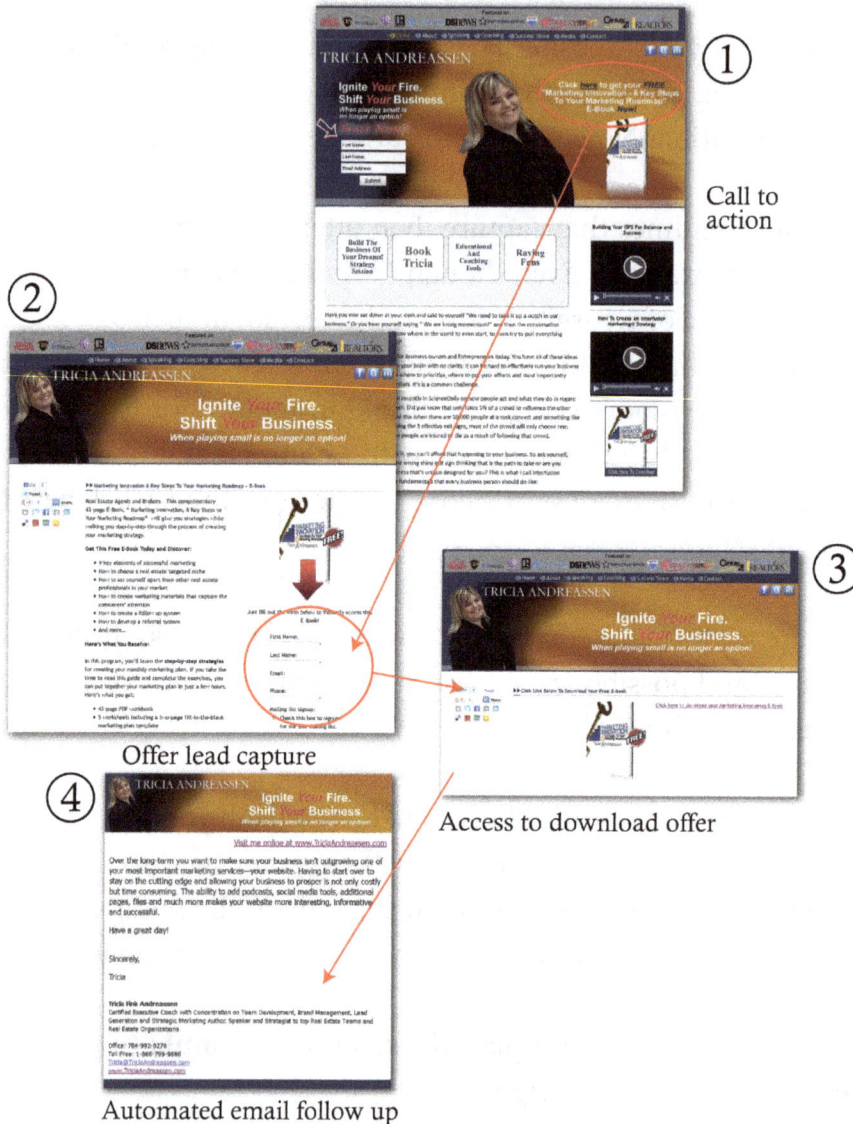

① Call to action

② Offer lead capture

③ Access to download offer

④ Automated email follow up

Calls to action should change with market trends. For example, at different times I have helped coach my clients to set up calls to action for:

Real Estate:

First time homebuyers - *"Trying to decide what route to take? Register now to evaluate the rent vs. buy spreadsheet. Know your numbers instantly here at www. BuyMyFirstHomeNow.com."*

Move-up homebuyers – *"Feeling out of room in your current home? Maybe it's time to move up? Click here."*

Short sales – *"Facing foreclosure? A short sale may be an option. Click here."*

Military – *"Getting transferred to another military base and trying to figure out your rent vs. buying options? Click here."*

Financial Planners:

Set up a college fund for your child's future – *"Seven steps to saving and being ready for college. Register now for this free Ebook that makes it happen."*

Retirement – *"Five ways to prepare for retirement – click here for the checklist!"*

General - *"Need a Financial Plan? Click here to get started now."*

Executive Coaches:

CEO's – *"Five key steps on how to build a sustainable team with your vision in mind – download this report now www.CEOVisionReport.com."*

Management – *"17 ways to build middle management teams – download this free Ebook at www.ManagementPrinciplesForGrowth.com."*

Hiring/HR – "*Three steps to effectively using profile assessments in the hiring process. Download this free report now at www.HireForTheirStrength.com.*"

And so forth . . . .

💡 **This is a critical piece of your strategy. Calls to action offer tools and education to answer your prospect's question or solve their problem.**

Offers that Engage

💡 **To be successful with calls to action, you should understand your targets and create calls to action that truly speak to them.**

Think back to Section I of this book, when you profiled your clients and your target market. What do they want from you? Provide it for them!

Offering information, guidance and tools can help you serve your potential customers' needs, while capturing their information. Here are some examples of resources and reports that can engage the consumer:

1. **Five steps to prepare your yard for an outdoor kitchen and pool**
2. **Three point checklist for fertilizing your yard in the fall**
3. **Ten ways to throw a successful tailgate party**
4. **Seven steps to financial independence after divorce**
5. **Four costly mistakes when it comes to your 401k plan**

In order to access these useful Ebooks and tools website visitors will need to perform one of the actions you have requested or give you the information you noted. Various offers will automatically appeal to different market groups, so you can ask for different actions and engagements depending on which offer your visitors choose.

What are some of the challenges, frustrations or desires my target market has that I can help them with?

_____

_____

_____

_____

_____

_____

_____

What are some resources, reports or other offers I can provide?

_____

_____

_____

_____

_____

_____

_____

Is there another service or tool that could be useful to one or more of my target groups? (e.g. a live chat option, discounts with home cleaners, etc.)

_____

_____

_____

_____

_____

_____

_____

How can I incorporate specific calls to action into my website? In which sections can I place them for maximum effect?

_____

_____

_____

_____

_____

_____

_____

Final Thoughts

☑ **Have on hand three to five calls to action for each niche within your target market.**

☑ **Sprinkle** *at least one* **call to action in every marketing campaign.**

☑ **Always have offers that are interesting and unique.**

☑ **Have an email follow-up campaign for every person in your database.**

Determining Your Business DNA

Having call to actions and unique offers is like **Sugar**.

It fuels the lead generation to grow your business.

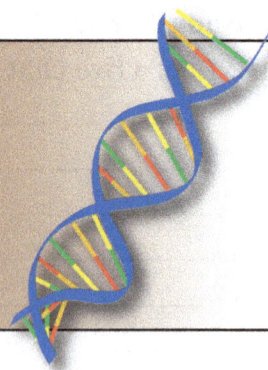

Lead Follow Up, Management and Conversion

You've generated the lead and got them interested but only 50% of the work is done. The secret ingredient is to be positioned in front of them while they are researching and to mentally connect with them while they are in the transaction process.

This is why we have to lead with education first and then provide plenty of opportunities and methods so they can ask questions or get in touch.

A study by the National Association of Sales Executives revealed that 48% of sales people never follow up on leads even once. Only 10% of salespeople make three contacts or more—but 80% of sales don't even happen until the fifth contact or beyond! Are you losing sales by not following up with your prospects? Without a doubt! How can you lock in more of those leads?

You have to create a great relationship by establishing a consistent follow-up system.

Email drip campaigns

Even once you have captured registration, be mindful that they may not be ready to move forward yet. As they are looking, you will want to use email follow-up to provide useful information, market statistics, and the calls to action we discussed in the previous section. This continues to position your name in front of them, so that by the time they are ready, you are the top-of-mind specialist they're going to call.

In 2011, MIT studied lead management using data from Inside Sales. They found that how fast you follow up with a lead makes a massive difference in whether you get the sale. The odds of contacting your lead decrease by ten times in the first five minutes, and the odds of "qualifying" the lead (having them be willing to go to the next step with you) decrease by over six times in the first hour.

It's crucial that, as soon as a lead comes in, you are immediately following up. Otherwise, they may have contacted your competitor too, and if they follow up first you have lost the lead.

I can hear you saying, "There's just no way I can contact every single lead in the first hour, let alone in the first five minutes!" Okay, so maybe you can't. But with an automated system, you can send them an email to follow up. That's why you have to have an automated system for adding leads to your database, so they can be acted on immediately.

Lead Follow Up Time That Convert To Contracted

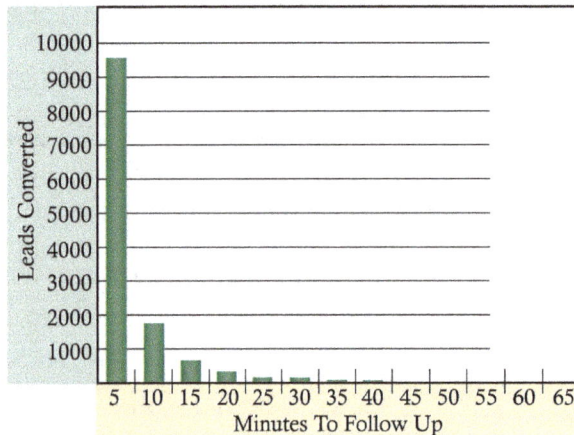

Once the leads are in your system, go through and organize them into groups depending on their interest. Sign them up for specific campaigns, and make notes about them for future reference. Make sure they are getting an experience that matches their interests and needs.

1. Make a list of where all your leads come from.

_____
_____
_____
_____
_____
_____
_____

2. Who receives all the leads (name and email of the person who sees the lead first in your business) once they are generated?

_____
_____
_____
_____
_____
_____
_____

3. Which of the lead sources from above get into an email follow up campaign?

_____
_____
_____
_____
_____
_____

What happens after a lead comes in.

Incorporating Phone Follow-Up

1. As soon as possible after that lead comes in, make a personal phone call to thank them for visiting your website and ask if there's anything you can help them with. You need to do this on the same day the lead comes in!

2. If you're interested in finding out more about how to approach different types of leads, contact me to ask about phone scripts and other training opportunities.

How long does it take for you to follow up on a lead with a personal call?

_____

_____

_____

_____

_____

_____

_____

Are you happy with that?

☐ Yes

☐ No

What could you do differently to improve that number?

_____

_____

_____

_____

_____

_____

_____

"The longer you wait to call them the less chance you have of getting the customer. They are impacted by the speedy response. They are often shocked when I call and by then they are already hooked because of your speedy response. In this industry that's very important. I promise if I don't get in touch with them in the first day they won't call me back. Even if they don't answer our speedy response I leave a detailed message telling them when I will call them back and that gives them one more chance, but if I don't get them on the first day, my percentage is cut in half."

Purvis Anderson
Owner of Skeeter Pro
www.SkeeterPro.com

Email Blasts, Newsletters, Special Offers, other ways to cultivate the relationship

1. The other way to contact people is the "blast" method, where you send out an announcement that reaches everybody with news they might want to hear. For example, let's say you've got an amazing new property that just came on the market, and you want to give your buyer list the inside scoop. Log into your email system, plug in a quick message with the information, and send it to everybody on your buyers list.

2. On the other hand, you might have a big announcement like a new referral

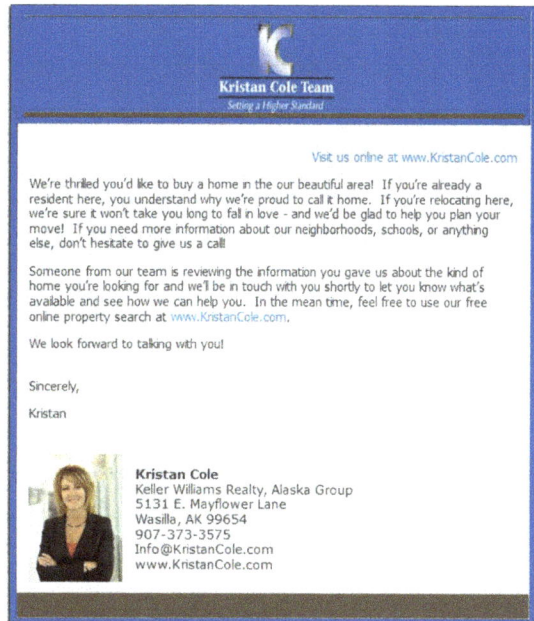

Visit us online at www.KristanCole.com

We're thrilled you'd like to buy a home in the our beautiful area! If you're already a resident here, you understand why we're proud to call it home. If you're relocating here, we're sure it won't take you long to fall in love - and we'd be glad to help you plan your move! If you need more information about our neighborhoods, schools, or anything else, don't hesitate to give us a call!

Someone from our team is reviewing the information you gave us about the kind of home you're looking for and we'll be in touch with you shortly to let you know what's available and see how we can help you. In the mean time, feel free to use our free online property search at www.KristanCole.com.

We look forward to talking with you!

Sincerely,

Kristan

Kristan Cole
Keller Williams Realty, Alaska Group
5131 E. Mayflower Lane
Wasilla, AK 99654
907-373-3575
Info@KristanCole.com
www.KristanCole.com

program, or a Thanksgiving pie giveaway, that you want to send out to your entire sphere of influence. When you send this message, you can simply select all your mailing lists at once, and reach hundreds of people with a single click.

3. Switching to email newsletters can also create huge savings. Kristan Cole discovered that she saved about $12,000 for her business by dropping direct-mail newsletters and switching to email delivery.

Branding Your Emails

1. Use the Interfusion approach! Your emails should have a similar look and feel to your website and every other piece of your marketing. Tie it all together to make sure your contacts are getting the full experience of your brand.

Does your email system allow for visual branding and the ability to customize mailing lists?

_____

_____

_____

_____

_____

_____

_____

What are some ways can you incorporate your brand into email messages?

_____

_____

_____

_____

_____

_____

_____

Final Thoughts

☑ **Know where all your leads are coming from and organize them into different groups for unique email campaigns.**

☑ **Time is money. The faster you follow up on the lead the better the conversion rate.**

☑ **Blend email follow up with phone follow up for maximum results.**

Determining Your Business DNA

Having a system for lead management and follow up is like **Nitrogen**.

It is a core element to a solid structure of success.

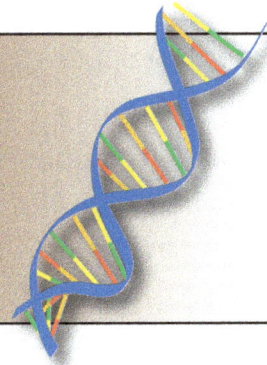

Pulling it All Together – Interfusion Worksheet

Building Your Website Navigation and Strategy

Recently, a client came to me worried. She wanted to add new pages to her website, but as a small operation she did not have lots of time or money to spend on updates. "Will I ever catch up with my competition?" she asked me. "Another company really has my market cornered. Will I ever actually be able to compete?"

"Don't worry!" I told her. "Go back and really research your market. Look in depth at where your sales are coming from and how much of the market your competitor has." And do you know what she found? Her competitor only had 17% of the sales in her market. She had created her own perception of what the competition had against her, but by learning more about her market, she saw it was not accurate. This also enabled her to find the "low hanging fruit"—the specific niches where she could improve her website and see a measurable difference almost immediately.

Which specific niche markets or geographic areas are easy to start working right away?

_____

_____

_____

_____

_____

_____

_____

Which ones will I start planning for?

_____

_____

_____

_____

_____

_____

_____

Website Appearance

What changes can I make on my homepage and on the interior pages (fonts, colors, photo elements and logo) to bring a stronger brand image to my overall presentation?

_____

_____

_____

_____

_____

_____

_____

Website Content

Start developing your website navigation; your blueprint of what you would like your website to have.

_____

_____

_____

_____

_____

_____

Uncover what content pages you want overall in your site.
Content page: A content page could be a page about a specific niche or geographic market you service.

What content page do I want to add to my website to solve my visitors' problem?

_____

_____

_____

_____

_____

_____

_____

Should this content page be a main button in my navigation or should it be a subpage (drop down menu) under the main button?

☐ Main Navigation   ☐ Subpage Under "Button/Main Content Name"

What call to action could I have on this content page that would promote lead capture as well as give the visitor something of immediate value?

_____

_____

_____

_____

_____

_____

_____

Once they register, what email group do I want this visitor to go into? What kind of email campaign should this visitor receive?

_____

_____

_____

_____

_____

_____

_____

Repeat this sequence for each content page you want to add in your site.

This will allow you to craft navigation like this example from a doctor's office:

- **Home**
- **Schedule an Appointment** – go to a page with a response form – allow them to subscribe to our monthly newsletter.
- **Service Areas** (this would be the main button/content page) – Button with content about the market areas we service to aid in Search Engine Optimization. Pages below will be about each market area so that search engines pick up this targeted content. Throughout this section feature mapping tools from each town to our office locations:
  - Jonesville (this would be the subpage) – Page about our helping patients in each of these markets.
  - Smithtown
  - Lakeville
- **Services** (this would be the main button/content page) – Button with content about the services patients can get help with. Pages below will be about the types of services so that search engines pick up this targeted content.
  - Physical Therapy – content page about our Physical Therapy treatments with

testimonials and call to action about "Physical Therapy vs. Surgery – Click Here to Download this Special Report."

- Surgical Procedures
- Ultra Sound
- **Diabetic Care**
  - Orthodics
  - What to look for
  - Ongoing therapy
- **Heal Pain**

From this exercise what changes can I make right away to my website navigation?

_____

_____

_____

_____

_____

_____

_____

How can I incorporate calls to action with special offers to promote lead capture?

_____

_____

_____

_____

_____

_____

_____

Email Follow-Up

How can I improve my system for capturing email addresses?

_____
_____
_____
_____
_____
_____
_____
_____

How do I want to start processing new email leads?

_____
_____
_____
_____
_____
_____
_____
_____

How can I improve my email drips to stay on contacts' radar?

_____
_____
_____
_____
_____
_____
_____
_____

Final Thoughts

☑ **Keep building your website navigation to attract your audience's attention.**

☑ **Don't underestimate the strength of a powerful call to action. Create unique offers to compel your visitors to further steps.**

☑ **Always make sure that every lead capture element in your website is "hooked up" to an automated email follow up campaign.**

☑ **Want to raise your lead conversion? Partner phone follow up with your email follow up campaign.**

Determining Your Business DNA

Focusing on your website marketing is like **Phosphate**.

The energy you put into the process will fertilize your business for years to come.

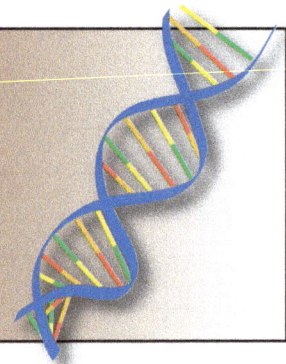

SECTION IV

Driving Traffic

The Non-Negotiable Strategy

Imagine you just bought a beautiful house in a great neighborhood. It's got everything you ever wanted: granite countertops, a Viking stove, beautiful crown molding, and a fully landscaped front yard.

Now imagine, once you move in, you stop mowing the lawn. In fact, you stop keeping the yard neat and tidy at all. The grass gets shaggy and full of weeds. The trees die. The gutters, which you never clean, get full of gunk that runs down the side of the house. After a couple of years, what do you think will have happened to your home's attractiveness and value?

It sounds crazy, but many people treat their website and their business this way. I see it all the time: you invest in an amazing site, and then you never maintain it. In this day and age, if you're treating your website like a finished product instead of constantly maintaining and improving it, it doesn't matter how well you run the rest of your business. You will not be getting the results you want.

Get in the Lead Generation Mindset

"My web and overall marketing strategy is a living, breathing thing," Linda Hall often says. As a client, she is an inspiration to work with because she truly lives in the mindset of generating leads, all the time. Even though I am very proud of the website that my company, Pro Step Marketing and Advertising, built for Linda, she and I are always working together to come up with new ideas. We ask ourselves: How do we get even more eyeballs looking at this site? How do we create interest and influence people to visit the site, engage with it, and interact with Linda's team?

On the other hand, I sometimes hear from clients who are disappointed by their SEO performance. "I used to rank so high on search engines," they say to me. "Now

I'm dropping. What gives?" As someone who knows web strategy inside and out, I can usually guess what is happening. The business leader isn't investing in analyzing, growing and improving their site, and it is getting stale.

Have you ever worked out a lot to get in great shape? What happens? For most of us, we get to a point where we feel amazing, and then we slack off a little bit. After a little while, those defined muscles go away. That's fine, if you happen to be married to somebody who loves you no matter what you look like. But if you're trying to meet attractive people and you haven't been keeping yourself in shape, you're going to have to work a little harder than the person who's been putting in the time at the gym on a regular basis.

In my classes and webinars, there is one big message I always want people to walk away with: Your website is never "finished." You can't just put it online and say, "VOILA! Now I don't ever have to do anything again." I know, that sounds extreme, but you would be surprised how often I see folks doing just that. "If you build it, they will come?" That really is a dream. You have to keep working on maintenance, strategy, upkeep and generating more leads.

Lead generation is a term that gets overused, but it has a simple definition: Lead generation is anything that makes the email arrive and the phone ring.

How do you make that happen? There are countless ways, but if your email and phone aren't presenting you with new business, your lead generation strategy isn't working.

You want them to remember you above your competition and you want to generate real business.

When we talk about driving traffic to your website, we're really talking about what happens *after* you get

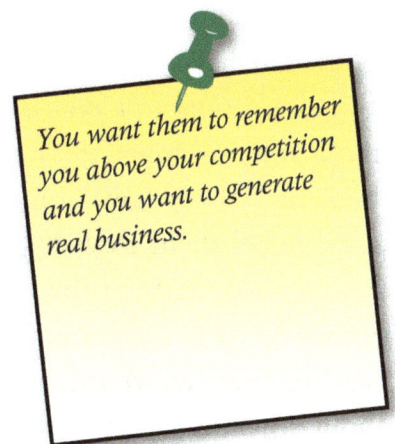

the traffic moving. You're doing all this because you want a specific result: You want the email. You want the phone calls. You want to get solid leads, so you can continue to succeed and thrive.

Here's the thing, however: People just don't pick up the phone as much anymore. Before they call or visit you, they're going to research you online. Knowing that truth, ask yourself: What will they find?

That's the non-negotiable strategy: You must constantly work to generate more leads through your website. Lead generation needs to be a part of your everyday life.

Practice Lead Generation Every Day

To succeed and grow, you must continually innovate and create new ways to drive traffic to your site. If you're not an inherently innovative person, then join up with a company like mine that has developed our own innovations for you to plug and play.

If you were to ask me, "Tricia, how much time should I be investing into this?" I couldn't honestly tell you a specific amount of time. It could be an infinite amount, because every activity that you do should have an end result of driving traffic to your site. Going to a restaurant for dinner, and run into a referral contact? The business card you give them had better have something on the back that will compel them to visit your site where they can download something that helps them. Have a new service for your customers? Direct people to visit a page on your site where they can get a special report about how this service can help them.

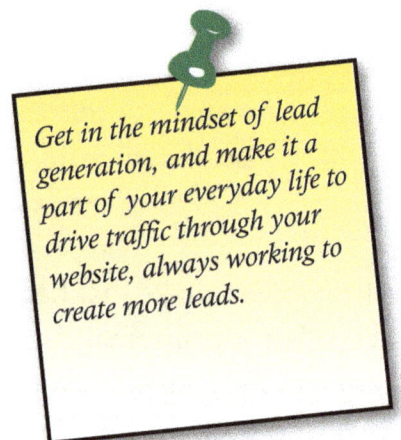

Get in the mindset of lead generation, and make it a part of your everyday life to drive traffic through your website, always working to create more leads.

Whatever you touch in the everyday world of work should have a caveat: "Is this driving traffic to my site?" Like getting up in the morning and brushing your teeth, it should be a part of your routine.

Look back to the Table Test you did in Section I of this book. Where can you improve your consistency in regard to driving more traffic to your website?

_____

_____

_____

_____

_____

_____

_____

What are three ways you can incorporate lead generation into your daily life?

1.

_____

_____

2.

_____

_____

3.

_____

_____

Practice Interfusion Marketing

Once you get really clear on who you are, what you represent and what makes you unique, that's when it gets *fun*.

💡 **Now you can practice the Interfusion Marketing strategy: mix and match, try different strategies and create your own marketing blend.**

Let's say you have a new financial program that would help your client be ready for retirement five years earlier than the original goal. This is a great program, and you decide to create a marketing recipe that will drive traffic to a landing page showcasing that offer.

1. On Monday, you do a direct mail campaign to the surrounding farming areas, to catch the attention of potential customers in the Smithtown community.
2. On Tuesday, you post the offer on Craigslist to the geographic market you want to generate business in, focusing on some of the great features that will attract that demographic.
3. On Wednesday, you promote it on Facebook with a call to action graphic and a link driving them back to where they can register for the offer. You use the Facebook marketing tactics of advertising this offer to a particular age group that lives in a targeted location.
4. On Thursday, you post a quick video on YouTube talking about the challenges that folks have when preparing for retirement. You focus on the worry this market has about having enough money in the bank to make those decisions, with a message at the end of the video and a clickable link to the landing page: "I have developed this special Ebook that will help you prepare for your retirement and be ready to live your dream in less than five years. Log on to www.YourTargetedURL.com."

The important part is this: Your marketing should always lead people back to your website, and it should always be generating new leads.

Case Study: Kristan Cole

Why does Kristan Cole floor the competition? Because she truly gets the concept of Interfusion Marketing. When the average Realtor gets a listing, he or she might say, "Okay, I'm going to get this on Facebook because that's where I market myself." Or, "I'm going to use a YouTube video for this, because my tour company makes one for me." But look at Kristan Cole, and she's doing Craigslist plus YouTube, radio, classified ads, Search Engine Optimization, email newsletters and so much more. She is constantly blending strategies to drive traffic. She's got the Interfusion Marketing mindset!

All four of these are effective. They all share the same DNA because the fundamentals are there to promote your marketing. The Interfusion is the working of different strategies to get results.

Kristan Cole and her team gather regularly and exhaust every idea they can imagine to drive more traffic. They ask themselves, "How do we reach more people and engage them? Where do we find people, and how do we get their attention?" They know the answer is never one simple thing. It's a blend of strategies, but it's always done consistently, with one thing in mind; to drive exposure for their business.

When was the last time you tried a new strategy for generating leads? What went right and what went wrong?

_____

_____

_____

_____

_____

_____

How can you blend strategies next time to drive more leads through your website?

_____

_____

_____

_____

_____

_____

💡 Final Thoughts

☑ **Treat your strategy as if it is ever evolving.**

☑ **Don't be shy about incorporating new things into the mix.**

☑ **Evaluate and track the results.**

Determining Your Business DNA

The Non-Negotiable Strategy is like **Phosphate**.

Once your website and your branding are in place, it's all about how much you can invest into getting the most from them. Fertilize your business and watch it grow!

Offline Marketing in an Online World

Offline marketing can be powerful if combined with your online marketing and web presence. Are you leveraging that power?

> *"We choose direct mail to advertise in neighborhoods where we know our service is highly desirable to those homeowners. Our mosquito spraying is something that people need in heavily wooded neighborhoods so we combine a special first time offer so they can learn about our services and see how it works. It allows us to focus on building our long term client base."*

Purvis Andreassen
Owner of Skeeter Pro
www.SkeeterPro.com

Get to the Fridge, not the Trash

I remember a while back going to the mailbox and getting a postcard that caught my attention. It was from Hair Club for Men. Why did it catch my attention? My husband will openly share that it has been a topic of conversation at many of our tailgate parties among friends. The conversation goes: "When you wear your hat, you look 15 years younger!" They all laugh because hair loss is something that many men (including my husband) face and it is a challenge for them; a topic of conversation.

If you only knew how many baseball hats Kurt owns, you would understand why this marketing piece caught my eye. The postcard had a picture of a guy behind the wheel of a car wearing a baseball hat. The call to action was "Discover life without the hat." That struck a chord with me: Not long before, my husband and I had gone on our anniversary trip, and he wore his baseball cap the whole time. He kept taking it off, saying "It's so hot!" But then he'd put it back on. Why? "I look cuter in the hat!"He'd say, "I look younger."

The five second rule

That mailer stuck with me, because it spoke to a real issue I knew my husband could identify with. I carried it into the house and I had a choice: Put it in the trash to my right, or hang it on the fridge to my left? It went on the fridge.

The five second rule applies with your offline marketing as well. If you only have a few critical seconds to make an impression, how can you get to the fridge instead of winding up in the trash? You need to provide a compelling reason for people to want to find out more.

Offline Marketing to Power Your Web Strategy

When you send out direct mail, run an ad in the paper, have a branded vehicle with your ad on it or drop door hanger ads on a front stoop what is your ultimate goal? It's to turn your activities into future sales. As we've previously talked about, that means that every single activity you do should be designed to drive lead generation through your website. Offline marketing is fuel for your online pipeline. The trick is to capture people's attention and get them to visit your website, engage with you, and ultimately sign up to get on your email list.

That's absolutely not negotiable.

💡 **If your offline marketing is not funneling people to your website, don't bother.**

Save your money and go on vacation instead. Don't even put out the postcard if you have no:

1. Call to action.
2. Unique offer.
3. That satisfies the need.
4. And funnels into an automated email follow up campaign.

Just don't do it.

Call to action

ShaneTWhiteSellerBook.com

Let's Try Your Table Test Now

Conduct the table test with a fresh approach. Is there a call to action to compel customers to want to get more information and in turn give you the ability to capture their contact information?

_____
_____
_____
_____
_____
_____
_____

Which of the calls to action and offers on your website could you link to offline promotional campaigns?

_____
_____
_____
_____
_____
_____
_____

In the past, what types of direct mailings have worked best? Does this connect to what you have learned about your market niche?

_____
_____
_____
_____
_____
_____

When was the last time you promoted a listing/service/product with direct mail? What were your results?

_____

_____

_____

_____

_____

_____

_____

What could you do to promote your listing differently than a competitor might advertise their listing?

_____

_____

_____

_____

_____

_____

_____

What are three action items you could do in your offline marketing efforts to generate more buyer interest?

_____

_____

_____

_____

_____

_____

The Interfusion Approach

When you've got something big and important to promote, never limit your options. You can't market only online or only offline, because trends are constantly shifting. Use the Interfusion method, and think of creative new ways to advertise! Interfusion means using different channels to expose your marketing message so it's not about doing one thing and stopping there.

It's about combining different tactics together to get more results.

One big hurdle for many is that direct mail doesn't always work right away. You might do a 200-piece mailing, and get no leads immediately. But how do you know that a few of your postcards didn't make it to the fridge, and that you won't get a call a few months later when your prospective customers are ready? It happens all the time.

Consistency is key. A consumer must be exposed to a brand or message several times before it will sink into their brain. If you just send one mailing and put up a website, you might get a response but you might not. You might be tempted to give up and say it didn't work. But studies show that it takes five to seven times for a consumer to have something imprinted on their brain enough to connect to the message and then take action. If you go about your campaigns strategically and with consistency, you will get the results.

It can be better to send out 500 pieces five times, than to send 5,000 in one fell swoop.

Be consistent, be patient, and spread your message across multiple marketing channels. If you follow the Interfusion guidelines, you will succeed.

$1 ▶ $12⁵⁷

$1 ▶ $12.57

Direct Marketing Association research finds every **$1** spent on direct mail generates, on average, **$12.57** in sales

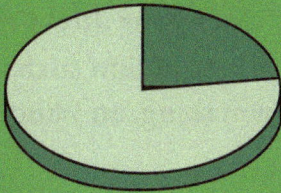

76%

According to the Exact Target Channel Preference Study:
76% of consumers have been directly influenced to purchase through direct mail

3/4

The USPS Postal Bulletin 22312 states that:
3 out of **4** people say they open and read direct mail

80%

According to the USPS Mail Moment Survey:
80% of people look at their mail daily

63% of mail is kept as least 2 days

Final Thoughts

☑ **Target who you are talking to – Know your Audience!**

☑ **So you collected the email addresses—what are you planning to do with them? Always follow up with an email drip campaign, to keep your relationship fresh and continue positioning yourself as the expert.**

☑ **Do the table test with the purpose of looking at your offline marketing and evaluating the power of driving them to your website. Does your direct mail give something more than just brand visibility? Add calls to action such as a coupon for your business, a checklist to use for decision making, an Ebook to see how they can achieve their goals.**

☑ **Don't just do one mailing and think it is going to penetrate your market. Have a sequential campaign to incorporate a series of touches in your market. I recommend a minimum of four mailings at least every 30 days.**

☑ **Track the results of your efforts so you can tweak or duplicate the strategy.**

Determining Your Business DNA

Offline Marketing is like **Sugar**.

This is pure fuel! Its sole purpose is to add power and drive to your website lead generation. With great offline marketing, your leads will take off!

Use Online Channels to Drive More Traffic

Social Media: What's it all about?

When my son, Jordan, was about five years old, he started playing soccer on his very first team. I remember watching his team play, and honestly it was hilarious. They had no strategy, of course. Wherever the soccer ball went, all eight bodies followed it in a cluster, bumping into each other and falling over. The only thing they could think to do was to follow each other, and they were all stuck to that ball.

After a couple of years of playing soccer, I noticed Jordan and his teammates were really starting to play their positions. They moved the ball down the field as a team, each position performing its role. They had learned to work a strategy. And just like I loved watching that soccer team evolve and succeed, I love watching businesses really begin to implement strategy in their marketing.

Don't take it the wrong way, but sometimes business people can seem to act like my son's first soccer team. They just follow the ball like everyone else. They don't follow a strategy that will work. That's a common behavior you may see at a conference where an idea from another business person on stage shows great promise. All of a sudden they drop the focus on something that might be foundational to their business, only to follow the "shiny" new trend. Karen Storey (who happens to also be my awesome sister!) and I were talking the other day about how the syndrome can distract business people from focusing on what actually brings the best results. She said "Just because it's new doesn't mean it's better."

Social Media should be a compliment, not be a replacement for other marketing tactics.

Adding Social Media to Your Strategy

A lot of business owners may say to themselves, "I'm going to do this social media campaign and not worry about my website right now. If I just do social media who cares about my website? My website is good enough." But ask yourself, "Is it really?"

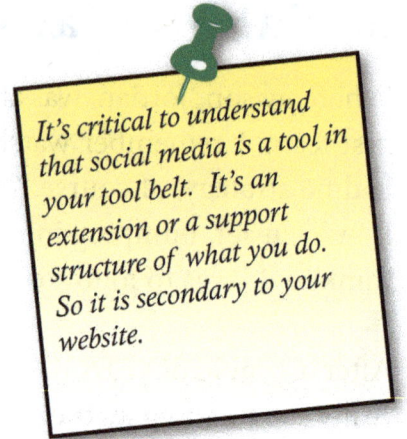

Social media is a tool in the tool belt. It's an extension or a support structure of what you do and it should be a support structure of your website.

It's critical to understand that social media is a tool in your tool belt. It's an extension or a support structure of what you do. So it is secondary to your website.

Every bit of marketing you do including social media should support your overall strategy, with the focus of driving customers back to your website.

Social media is a breeding ground for hot new trends but when you step back and really take a look, you can see that it's only one piece of a complete marketing strategy, and that a great strategy lasts longer than any trend.

Have you previously coordinated promotional campaigns between your web marketing and your social media? What was the result?

_____

_____

_____

_____

_____

_____

What is one call to action you have identified for your website that you also want to promote via social media?

_____

_____

_____

_____

_____

_____

_____

Personal vs. Professional Social Media Profiles

If you don't have a coordinated social media campaign to drive your social media content, what are you actually planning to post? Photos of your pet? If you are creating the image of a successful business, then professional marketing campaigns are key to strengthening that image and validating you as an expert.

By the same token, you must avoid being too professional in a personal space. For example, let's say you have a friend from church who is a teacher and has no real interest in financial planning. You invite them over to your house for a barbecue—and when they arrive, you spend the next three hours telling them about why they need a plan and what can happen if they don't have one. Do you think they'll leave your house saying, "Wow, that was fun and I can't wait to go back?" It is doubtful.

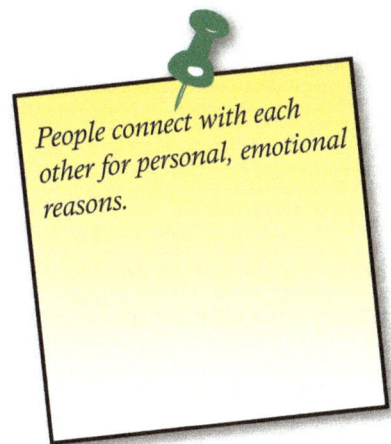

People connect with each other for personal, emotional reasons.

People use social media to create relationships, to bond with each other and to experience emotional connections. In that atmosphere, you can be a three-dimensional person: not just your business, not just your photos, but a real person that might post updates on your day and details of your everyday life. In that context, if you start bombarding your friends with market conditions, they're going to be turned off very quickly.

It's okay to sprinkle in some information about work on your personal page, but your job is not the reason most people have you as a friend. That's why it's a good idea to create a professional profile that is separate from your personal presence. Social media is constantly changing, but for the past several years, Facebook has been a dominant force. Most businesses now have official pages on Facebook. It allows you to build your brand, and showcases you as a viable, creditable business.

Do you create separate social media profiles for your business and personal pursuits? How do you use them differently?

_____
_____
_____
_____
_____
_____

How many times per week do you post on your personal social media? How many times on your business page? Do you ever post the same thing to both pages?

_____
_____
_____
_____
_____

Although there are many different social media marketing channels, let's focus on the three most popular that can make a huge impact on your business.

✓ **Facebook**

✓ **LinkedIn**

✓ **YouTube**

Facebook: It's not just for kids anymore!

Facebook is one of the most popular social media channels. Most of us have a private profile on Facebook. It's just where the world is today. At the time of this writing, however, if you know anyone under the age of 16, they would probably say Facebook is no longer cool and now it is Instagram. Social media is always changing, but for the moment Facebook is still a dominant part of our culture. Social media channels like Facebook are a huge part of our culture. It's about connecting, creating relationships and bonding between people. That's what people desire. They often go to Facebook to fill an emotional need or just to feel a connection. This is why it is important to understand the DNA of why people use Facebook and be aware of its impact on your business.

Facebook Stats

42% Marketers say Facebook is critical to their business

75% Increase over last 3 years for the number of businesses who say Facebook is critical

62% Marketers say social media has become more important in the last 6 months

73% Companies acquired B2C customers from Facebook

43% Companies acquired B2B customers from Facebook

80% US social network users prefer to connect with brands through Facebook

70% Say auto-posting to Facebook decreases likes and comments

facebook® Facts

1.5 Billion monthly active users

2.7 Billion likes per day

819 Million mobile users monthly

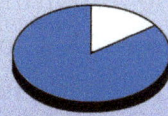

80% of daily active users are outside the U.S. and Canada

1 out of 5 web pages viewed by an internet surfer is a facebook page

699 Million daily active users on average

57% Female Users
43% Male Users

250 Million photos are uploaded daily

23% of the Facebook population visits the site 5 or more times daily

20 Mins. A Facebook user spends approximately 20 mins. per visit

Using Facebook to Improve Search Engine Results

If you want to capture another chance to perform well on search engines, make sure you have a strongly branded social media presence. If you create a business page on Facebook, it will soon appear on Google due to its ability to index. Now anybody searching for your name will pretty quickly end up on your Facebook business page. You are not likely to get the same results with a personal profile, where your private information is subject to more protection.

This works for capturing niche markets. As a case study, let's look at the strategy I put into place to reach a specific targeted group of Realtors who specialize in working short sales. I created a turnkey marketing system that included a website, lead capture reports and Ebooks, as well as direct mail pieces, craigslist ads, Facebook ads and more. Instead of promoting the product I decided to create a page that would engage the Realtor to like the page. We created a Facebook business page titled Short Sale Marketing, with the web address of www.Facebook.com/ShortSaleMarketing.

As I write this, I can Google "Short Sale Marketing," and guess what comes up? My company website ranks and my Facebook page. I am dominating two of the top three spots on Google! This business page creates an added opportunity to rank in search results. It cost nothing to set up the page and it continuously brings in leads.

I don't recommend creating a page like this for every single niche in your market unless you are dedicated and committed to posting actively and managing the page - but if you are actively looking to dominate a specific area, and are willing to invest a few hours per week, you can see real results from a strategy like this one.

Seven Ways To Turn Facebook Into A Lead Generating Machine

1. Have a photo on your page that helps build your brand and your connection to the audience.

2. Include Calls to Action on your page to get them back over to special offers on your website.

3. Integrate a Timeline Cover into your presentation that showcases your personality and the unique offer you can provide.

4. Include video on something relevant that relates to your market and include a link to the lead capture section in your site.

5. Use advertising tools like "Boost Your Post" to expose your posting to a wider audience than just people connected to you.

6. Run ads specific to the demographics of your target audience. You can drill down on these when you set up the ad and choose where they live, what ages will see the ad, and their specific interests or likes.

7. Craft ads that speak to that demographic or geographic market and drive them to your special offer.

Look back to the niche markets you have already identified. Is there one you would like to feature on a custom Facebook page?

LinkedIn – The Critical Element to Credibility

LinkedIn is a social media channel that should be at the top of your list. It's a wonderful way to build your brand, get found on the web, and improve your Google rankings. This is the business channel to showcase your expertise and prove your credibility.

You may have a LinkedIn profile out there, but it might not be showcasing your entire resume or the offerings that you have to give. The bottom line is: when somebody searches for your name, they may come across your LinkedIn profile first and want to see how you are representing yourself in a business capacity. This includes potential customers who are looking to hire you as their expert.

I highly recommend that you "beef up" your resume on LinkedIn. This is also a place where you can own your niche, tout your experience, and prove that you are the expert for your target market.

Are you an expert at leadership coaching and training? Do you specialize in employee evaluations or hiring? Do you have certifications that show you have advanced skills in a particular field? Mention it on your LinkedIn profile! Any credentials, designations, or other specific things that add to your credibility should be included here.

Get Recommendations on LinkedIn

Once you maximize your LinkedIn profile, it's time to go to work getting those recommendations. Recommendations are as powerful as testimonials in your website. **It should always be top of mind for you to generate testimonials and recommendations from your client base after you help them sell or purchase a property.**

You may already be in the habit of asking clients for a testimonial to put on your website, but don't forget that LinkedIn is another channel to showcase these references.

Here are the steps to get recommendations from your existing and past clients:

✓ **Ask them if they are on LinkedIn.**

✓ **Connect with them on LinkedIn.**

✓ **Ask them for a recommendation and offer that if they will provide one for you that you will reciprocate one for them. Even if you have not worked in a business capacity in their work environment, you can complement them on their attitude, attention to detail or organizational skills.**

When people see real recommendations from real people, it strengthens you as the expert. You become the professional of choice. You are seen from a different perspective due to what people are saying.

Ten Ways to Turn LinkedIn into a Lead Generating Machine

LinkedIn is the place to build your credibility in your niche while also connecting with like-minded business people. With many folks investigating your experience online, following are a few strategies to put into practice.

1. Have a separate profile for your business and for personal. Either page could be where they land first so make sure you fill out all sections to make a solid first impression.

2. Use a photo that is professional. This is not the place to show yourself on vacation or in a casual moment.

3. Make sure to get a branded URL for your profile. Go to the "public profile" section and create the URL that you would want to use in your marketing.

4. Write articles. Post the article in your website or blog and post it as a call to action on LinkedIn with a link back over to your site.

5. "Sprinkle in" Calls to Action in your posts that prospects to a landing page to capture the lead and provide them the unique offers.

6. Connect to other professionals in your industry in other geographic markets to keep a pulse on what is happening and build business referrals.

7. Ask for recommendations! Whether it is a colleague or a past client, this is a strong way to allow you to shine in the face of competition.

8. Design for SEO in mind. Add keywords to your profile page which allows for stronger indexing in a Google search or a specific search on LinkedIn.

9. Follow other companies that are in your industry or parallel to your overall business strategy. This can help you stay cutting-edge and unique in your offerings.

10. Showcase your skills and achievements. LinkedIn gives you the ability to list up to 50 skills in your profile so revisit this often to make sure you are leveraging your strongest skill in the network. Have a new certification or recent award? Don't forget to continually update your profile.

To set up your LinkedIn Profile you must have an email address that is branded to your company like www.yourname@company.com. Generic email addresses like gmail are not permissible.

Look at your resume, professional bio, business card – anything that lists your experience. Are all your credentials and skills being represented on your LinkedIn profile? What would you change?

_____

_____

_____

_____

_____

_____

_____

How else could you beef up your LinkedIn bio to tell the story of your expertise and mastery?

_____

_____

_____

_____

_____

_____

_____

How strong is your brand on LinkedIn? What are some ways you could improve it overall?

_____

_____

_____

_____

_____

_____

_____

Make a list of all your achievements, certifications and awards. What year were these accomplished?

_____

_____

_____

_____

_____

_____

_____

What are some things you learned about LinkedIn that could help you today in your business?

_____

_____

_____

_____

_____

_____

_____

Search for your name on the search engines (Google). Does your LinkedIn profile come up on the front page?

☐ Yes
☐ No

What could you do to improve your ranking and make your profile more search engine friendly?

_____

_____

_____

_____

_____

_____

_____

YouTube – The Evangelistic Megaphone

A YouTube channel is the most popular designation on the Internet for video creation and sharing. Are you harnessing this power to promote your business? If not, now is the time to jump on board and learn how to brand yourself as the expert on information that relates to your target market.

YouTube can enhance search engine rankings tremendously due to their algorithms. Your video content will actually be transcribed into content and will pick up keywords for the target market you are going after.

This could be a strong weapon in your marketing arsenal!

Eight Ways to Turn YouTube into a Lead Generating Machine

YouTube is not just for funny videos anymore. The Google power behind it is tremendous and allows you to connect in a unique way with your audience. Here are eight strategies that you can put into action right now:

1. Be mindful of what you set up for a username on your account. The user name determines the name of your channel and ultimately your channel URL. When choosing your username make sure to use your name or business with NO SPACES. Here is an example of mine: www.YouTube.com/InterfusionMarketing.

2. You may already own a YouTube channel for your business but now is the time to think outside of the normal and consider something that is consumer focused and deals with a specific niche or topic. You can sign up for a YouTube account from the website's homepage. Be sure to name the account exactly like the domain name you would want to advertise with all the words together and no spaces (WasillaRealEstate), making it easy for consumers to remember your address (www.YouTube.com/WasillaRealEstate).

3. Convert your blog article into a video. Optimum video length is two minutes but if you have more information to share keep it in the three to five minute range.

4. Include a call to action in your video as a clickable link to drive traffic to your landing page where you can get the lead and also use the link in your email follow up campaign.

5. Write a name for your video that is keyword rich for your niche and be deliberate in capitalizing the words. This is a SEO strategy.

6. The first 45 characters or so of your video title is displayed in the YouTube search on mobile so load this with keyword phases for SEO.

7. Power up your description. You want to compel the viewer to want to hit the "play" button. Put your call to action in the description. For example: Five ways to run a successful corporate retreat. In addition to the call to action, maximize the additional space to add a conversational, yet keyword rich, description.

8. Practice Interfusion! Blog about your video and leverage the video on your blog posting. In addition, add the call to action on your LinkedIn page with a link that takes them to your YouTube video which in turn takes them to your landing page.

What kinds of video could you put on YouTube that would promote your business, a special product or service?

_____

_____

_____

_____

_____

_____

_____

How could you include a call to action in your YouTube video that would drive prospects to a special offer and landing page?

_____

_____

_____

_____

_____

_____

_____

What channels could you create that would lend you to a specific niche market and speak to that specific audience?

_____

_____

_____

_____

_____

_____

_____

Use the Interfusion approach

Always keep in mind that your calls to action and campaigns will originate from your unique business DNA, plus the trends and conditions in your own specialized niche. Once you've created the campaigns you want to run, leverage your calls to action on social media just like any other marketing channel.

Don't be shy about trying new things. For example, many social media networks offer some type of advertising. Give it a shot, and see what happens. Or you might happen come across a network like Instagram, which only allows you to post images. Could you add your URL to the corner of your image, to drive traffic back to your site? Could you Tweet about your latest article, blog post or video? Think creatively about how you can incorporate the campaigns you already have, into new channels. Social media is constantly evolving, but you can find opportunities in any situation if you understand your basic DNA and the motivations of your target customers.

What is one way you could carry a campaign over to a new social channel?

_____

_____

_____

_____

_____

_____

_____

Final Thoughts

☑ **Incorporate Social Media marketing into your plan to evangelize your message.**

☑ **Different channels will reach different consumers. The key to success is using multiple strategies to relay your marketing message.**

☑ **Leverage your articles, calls to action and educational elements on social media postings with the strategy to drive prospects back to your site.**

Determining Your Business DNA

Social media marketing is like **Sugar**.

Everybody is on social media! Feed people's collective energy with exciting calls to action, and they will boost your business to new levels.

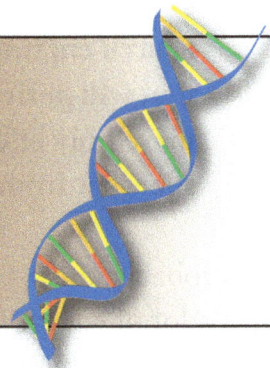

Search Engine Optimization (SEO)

What happens when you build a beautiful website and nobody sees it? That's right: nothing. In order for your website to be effective at bringing in leads and branding yourself as the expert in your field, that website needs to be easy to find. The vast majority of your potential customers are going to do a quick Web search and click on the first two or three real estate websites that appear in the results. If you want to capture those leads, you need to get to the top of that list!

Search engine optimization or SEO is the science of creating a website that will perform well and get top placement in search results. It can be incredibly effective. When I worked with Kristan Cole on her website, she went from having 14% of her sales come through her site to 40%.

As you probably know, SEO is actually a very complex process, and to do it expertly requires a lot of education and knowledge. I'm not going to teach you to be a SEO expert. Instead, I'm going to give you some ideas of things you can do right now, with the resources you should already have, to improve your web search results and create measurable changes in your website's effectiveness.

What Do Search Engines Want?

Part of the reason that SEO is so complicated is that people are always trying to game the system. Ever since the first search engine came out, website programmers have been pulling tricks to improve their rankings. Thankfully, all tricks aside, there are a few things you can do that are guaranteed to improve your ranking no matter *what*. Those things are:

1. **Solid, Unique Content:** When your website is rich in information, well organized and truly authoritative, it will always perform well with search engines. Just remember, you should never take content from another source with a quick cut and paste. The search engines are smart and will flag you for this tactic and it will not help you. Your content should always be unique to your site so that it builds market position and credibility.

2. **Creditable Inbound Links:** When other authoritative sites link back to yours, search engines understand that your site is trusted, and will give it a good ranking.

3. **Blogging:** When you are continually updating your site with new and current information, search engines know that your site is up-to-date and relevant, and will rank it above sites that do not update.

"Getting found on the web is extremely important. In today's world people are on their mobile and conducting a search possibly from their car and we want to be top of mind for them. If we are not online, we don't exist to those who don't know us yet. In the beginning when you helped me develop my strategy we talked about how to build sections on the geographic areas so that I rank for those specific keywords. My site is constantly being evaluated and I am able to see how people are finding us and what they are typing in to locate us. These tools allow me to stay aware of how to continually make additions to our site so that we rank highly. Right now we are number 2 on the Google for Lake Norman Coffee Shop. It can't get much better than that."

JR Hearld
Owner of Cabbellas Coffee Shop
www.CabbellasCoffeeShop.com

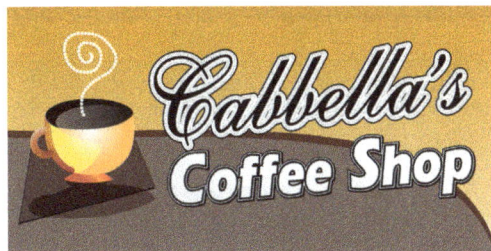

Your goal with content pages is to be *the* specialist in your area or your niche. Not only will a site with awesome content rank higher with search engines, but it will also convert more of your visitors into leads when they see your mastery of the market.

I could write a separate book on the ins and outs of creating awesome content pages. It is absolutely a science, but you are not in the content business. For that reason, I highly recommend that you work with a SEO professional on this. If you're great at writing content, you can do the writing yourself—or if you'd rather have somebody else do it, then make sure to hire a SEO expert with writing experience.

Right now, you can start to plan the areas of your site where you will expand and add content.

Look back to Section III of this book, where you determined your website navigation. Now, refresh your website navigation to include the <u>geographic areas you cover and those you want to start covering</u>. Use separate paper as needed.

_____

_____

_____

_____

_____

_____

_____

Interfuse your niche markets or area of specialty(ies) as separate content pages. How do they fit into your website's organization? How will visitors find them?

_____

_____

_____

_____

_____

_____

_____

Building Links

As discussed above, the more—and more authoritative—your inbound links are, the better your site will perform with search engines.

A few years back, search engines started paying a lot more attention to how many links your site had. When people found out, they started creating complex webs of sites, all linked to each other. However, many of the people using that technique were effectively creating spam sites that didn't add any content or value. Search engines responded by paying more attention to the *type* of site linked to yours.

If you have creditable, well known and established websites linked to your site, it can increase your performance in search engine results. That isn't as difficult as it sounds, nor is it easy.

One tactic that is very effective is press release distribution. With this method, create a press release every time you have a big announcement, and hire a distribution service to send it out. A certain percentage of the webmasters receiving your release will post it on their site. If you have made sure to include links to your site in the release, then all those sites are now going to be linked to you. These are creditable news organization sites and industry sites and because of that, they will work in your favor as far as the search engines are concerned.

Another tactic is to leverage the Chamber of Commerce and other community-oriented local websites, and ask them to link to you. If you have sponsored a local charity or event, make sure they add a link in exchange for your sponsorship. These links add up quickly, because each of them is worth a lot to search engines. You will see the difference very quickly in your website traffic!

Which local organizations have websites with information about your community?

_____

_____

_____

_____

_____

_____

_____

Which contacts do you have that might be willing to trade links with you?

_____

_____

_____

_____

_____

_____

_____

Which organizations and events have you been involved with?

_____

_____

_____

_____

_____

_____

Blogging

So many business owners don't understand the importance of having fresh, up-to-date information on their websites. "What happens if I write a blog and nobody reads it?" people ask me. "Google will read it!", I tell them. By updating your site regularly, you show search engines that you are providing current information.

Not only that, but you are adding more keywords to your site with every post. Every blog post is essentially adding a new page to your website, with information about your niche. The result: you will get more visitors with every article!

The key to blogging effectively is to keep it simple. You want it to be easy, and you probably don't have the time to write long feature articles. So come up with some simple ideas that you can write in less than an hour!

Circle the topics that you feel you can easily write about.

Why Massages Improve Your Health	**Financial News Updates**
Promoting Your Ebook	**Hiring For Growth**
Simple Repairs to Help Sell Your Home	**Building Your Retirement Portfolio**
Rent It or Flip It?	**Five Ways To Inspire Your Workforce**
The Danger of Mosquito Bites	**Local News**
Physical therapy or Surgery: Which Should You Choose?	**Fun Outings With Kids**
	Travel Tips For Visitors
How to Save on Energy Costs	
Five Ways To Run A Corporate Retreat	**Five Tips to Pricing Your Home Right**
Low/No Cost Marketing Ideas	**Webcam Feeds From Local Points of Interest**

Add your own blog topic ideas: (readers love numbers and lists – Five steps or three keys – so remember this when writing your blogs)

"If you try to build your site specifically around paying for clicks it will gain search engine position but the minute you stop it will fall. What I chose to do was to hire Tricia's company, to position me in a more progressive search engine position. Our website is in a much better position with this SEO content. We rank on the front page of the search terms for our target market. This is a strategy that we practice every day. Today you may have to do both pay-per-click while working an SEO strategy but SEO is critical to get the site where you want it to be and have it maintain stability."

Linda Hall
Century 21 First Choice
www.LindaHall.com
www.YourGuideToHomeSelling.com

Final Thoughts

☑ **Don't think that a blog alone is going to get you found on the Search Engines.**

☑ **A blog is not necessarily the "fix" to help prospects find you, it is a tool. Remember, a blog is simply an online journal of content. If you are not fully committed to writing a blog then it may not be the best route to take.**

☑ **Make sure the infrastructure of your site is built for SEO coding. Each page must be individually coded with Title Tags, Alt Tags, and descriptions.**

☑ **Avoid combining multiple topics on one page. Instead, have each subject have its very own page so that it is more indexable.**

☑ **If you want to rank for specific keywords, make sure you have pages on those keywords. For example, if you want to rank for Wasilla Real Estate have a page on Wasilla. If you also want to rank for luxury homes in Wasilla have an additional page on Luxury Homes. This creates the right blend for optimal leverage.**

Determining Your Business DNA

Search Engine Optimization is like **Phosphate**.

By incorporating the building blocks of your real estate DNA in a way that search engines can understand, you guarantee a growth in traffic and leads.

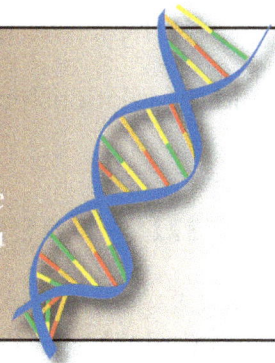

Landing Pages (Branded and Non-Branded)
VS. Stealth Websites

If you're really serious about driving traffic through your website, you've undoubtedly heard of stealth sites and landing pages. You may even be using them already. However, many of the business folks I work with are not totally clear on the differences and similarities between the two.

Are they the same, or are they different?

Landing pages and stealth sites have major similarities but are different in a couple of important ways. Basically, the reason behind having a stealth site or a landing page is to generate lead capture. That's really what we want the outcome to be. We want to:

1. Generate the lead.

2. Sort that lead into an email follow up campaign.

3. Prospect them over time.

4. Build the relationship and credibility.

Landing Pages

A landing page is a specific location, a one page layout that is designed with one thing in mind. This could be a page that is branded promoting you as the expert or non-branded (stealth) to be consumer focused.

A branded landing page focuses on getting visitors to engage with you while building your brand. They know who you are and what you

are about from your branded page. A non-branded landing page is purely to encourage lead capture and build your email database. It is usually informational or educational and deals with a specific subject matter. This type of site allows them to get more information on a particular subject.

This is one of the landing pages that I use to reach the real estate industry target market. This promotion drives visitors to register to attend the webinar. On the webinar I only discuss strategies that relate to the real estate industry.

I follow this formula for additional target markets like coaches, women entrepreneurs, and small businesses so that each message and conversation is specific to that niche market. Below is another landing page specific to the business and life coach target market.

New Webinar
7 Steps To Building Your Coaching Practice

Click HERE To Register!

Tricia Andreassen
Certified Executive Coach And Business Strategist

Wednesday Oct 23, 2013
1:00 PM - 2:30 PM EST

Looking to build your business and generate the type of clients you want to work with? Come to the webinar and learn how to:

- Attract a specific niche market
- Get clarity on your marketing message
- Build your brand and expertise
- Create website that connects to your visitor
- Leverage your database and build your pipeline
- And more!

Isn't it time to take coaching practice to a whole new level?

SIGN UP NOW!

Click Here To Register Now!

Share This Page

Like 0   Tweet 0

Use your Calls to Actions and Offers to Create a Compelling Landing Page

We have been focused on how to integrate calls to action with offers so you can engage potential customers. Those calls to action don't have to live exclusively on your website. You may see an opportunity or a trend in the market that will allow you to create a landing page specific to that topic while presenting yourself as the expert.

Take, for example, using an Ebook in your campaign. Now imagine that your visitors see an advertisement in the local publication or on a listing flyer that shows you are the expert providing the book of information. You instantly become the credible resource!

Your visitors would go directly to the page. They would download the Ebook (which is the offer that goes along with the call to action). As part of getting the offer, they would input their email address and then be placed into an email drip campaign. That's how a landing page works.

When using a branded landing page you want to be seen as the expert. You are not hiding who you are. You're being a bit blatant about it, in fact, so anybody coming to this site will know that you are the expert providing the information.

What Branded Landing Pages could you create to use in your strategy? What domain names would go with the landing page?

_____

_____

_____

_____

_____

_____

_____

Do you have an Ebook or another resource that you can use on a targeted landing page? If not, what could you offer on your landing page?

_____

_____

_____

_____

_____

_____

_____

A Non-Branded Landing Page Does Not Include any Branding

An example of a non-branded landing page eliminates your branding and focuses purely on their situation.

Stealth Websites – An Advanced Strategy

What do you think of when you use the word 'stealth'? Think about the military and how they use stealth bombers. They fly in the middle of the night. Nobody can see them. They are flying undercover to achieve a specific mission.

With a stealth site, you are flying undercover, and choosing not to display your identity. Like a stealth bomber, you are working to achieve a specific goal, rather than increase your own brand with this type of site. This is a full featured website that is not branded to focus on you, but instead focuses on a specific topic and a specific consumer.

The purpose of this strategy is to attract people who might not want to talk to you just yet, but they do want to get information on their terms and you can provide that.

This is a great example of understanding your target market. Even though landing pages can squeeze a lead capture form you want to be aware that some topics of conversation serve best with a fully designed website that helps that consumer make a decision. Once the consumer is at this site there are many lead capture locations that are positioned to provide real education to the visitor, from calculator tools to Ebook downloads and more.

> *"A few years ago we saw the trend in our market to help distressed sellers who were behind on their mortgages payments and were facing foreclosure. Instead of just having a landing page we understood that the seller may not want to come to our website but instead look for information on their own terms. This is when www.MyPrivateShortSale.com was born. This site is dedicated with loads of information to assist this specific type of client. With the continual shift in the market I now have a stealth site focused on for sale by owners and traditional sellers."*

Tamara Inzunza
RE/MAX Executives
www.VirginiaHomeSellingInfo.com

When to Use a Landing Page vs. a Stand Alone Stealth Site

Each of these strategies serves a great purpose. Both have their place in the world of marketing. Ideally, you will blend the two, using the Interfusion approach to drive more traffic and capture more leads.

1. For a branded landing page, you might take out an ad in the paper that says, "Have no Savings for Retirement? Put 30 years of experience in the financial planning industry to work for you. Get Joe Smith's Ebook at JoeSmithFinancialSecrets.com."

   Now, if a person is in the mode of immediate action then they will think of you and will know that you're the one supplying the information they are looking for.

2. For a Non Branded (Stealth) Landing Page let's say that someone is just starting to think about saving for the future. Practicing the Interfusion Marketing method you may want to run an ad on Facebook very focused on that one message. "If you were laid off tomorrow what savings would you have in place? Download your free Ebook and learn how to prepare for your future at www.YourFutureDoesMatter.com"

3. A stand alone (Stealth) website will allow you to market more extensively to a specific group. These are sites which fulfill more than a one-page registration form. They are deep and rich with targeted information about a specific topic. They are loaded with multiple calls to action that promote lead capture with multiple strategies behind it. If you have a business that can service multiple target audiences this is a great strategy. For example: My companies are diversified into different business markets. www.RealtyBizCoach.com is specifically designed to assist real estate professionals from all over the globe and provide online educational tools specific to this niche.

What Non-Branded (Stealth) Landing Pages could you create to attract a different target market? What domain names would go with those landing pages?

_____

_____

_____

_____

_____

_____

_____

What stand-alone (stealth) website could you create to use in your strategy to attract a different target market? What domain name would go with this site?

_____

_____

_____

_____

_____

_____

_____

Final Thoughts

☑ With landing and stealth pages, you begin your conversation already knowing what your new contact is looking for. That helps you lead with the right topic of conversation from the very beginning.

☑ Zero in on a very specific topic of conversation that is relevant to the market. You may find some of the topics are more suited for a short term strategy and some are better suited for a longer term timeline.

☑ Have a catchy domain that you can advertise through the different marketing channels so that you follow the Interfusion Marketing formula.

Determining Your Business DNA

Landing pages and Stealth sites like **Phosphate**.

They allow you to reach a multitude of niche markets with a targeted message resulting in growing your business.

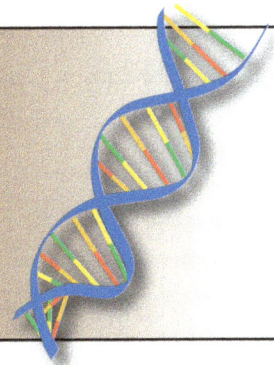

Pulling It All Together — Interfusion Worksheet

Drive Traffic To Your Business

By now, you know that the Interfusion marketing approach is all about combining and blending strategies to create the best possible results. You know that just because you're trying one tactic, that doesn't mean you ignore everything else. That understanding is central to how you drive traffic to your website.

Remember: Driving traffic is anything you do to make the email flow in and the phone ring.

Almost anything you can think of is worth trying, and the more ideas you try, the more success you will have. Provided you remain mindful of your business DNA in creating your strategy, you can engineer ongoing success in your niche.

That's Interfusion in a nutshell. Interfusion is taking a marketing message, getting clear on it, and evangelizing it across as many channels as possible. How can you adopt the Interfusion attitude in your own efforts to drive website traffic?

Step 1: Write down one call to action and an offer that can fill a need for your target market.

_____

_____

_____

_____

_____

Step 2: What domain name can you use to market that call to action?

_____

_____

_____

_____

_____

_____

_____

Step 3: Where could you advertise this domain name to drive traffic to a landing page? List ten ways:

1. _____

2. _____

3. _____

4. _____

5. _____

6. _____

7. _____

8. _____

9. _____

10. _____

Step 4: Where could this call to action be placed on your main website to generate lead capture?

_____

_____

_____

_____

_____

_____

_____

Step 5: What did you take away from this exercise?

_____

_____

_____

_____

_____

_____

_____

SECTION V

Interfusion Marketing in Action

I interviewed several business leaders of various industries for this book to help you see how everything should pull together to get the results you want. Notice how they are each doing unique things to market their business and also notice the *similar* things they are doing. These are the core fundamentals that you must use to build your own unique DNA.

Kristan Cole

Vice President MEGA Agent Expansion KWRI
National Educator, Speaker and Trainer
Keller Williams Realty, Alaska Group
www.KristanCole.com
www.AnchorageRealEstateListings.com
www.WasillaShortSales.com
www.AlaskaHomeSellingInfo.com

Kristan Cole with Keller Williams is practicing Interfusion Marketing and continuously follows a formula of success. We discussed Kristan's evaluation of her business and how that created her roadmap to success.

TRICIA: I'm excited about chatting with you since we have worked together for several years. I have looked through notes of the very first time we talked about your business. One of the first things you did was to meet with your team and look at your numbers. You evaluated the market in Wasilla at the time and now you have expanded into Anchorage as well. I want us to talk about that expansion and the new trends in the market. One thing that you really focused initially on was that 60% of the market was first time buyers but it has evolved over the years. You've seen trends and opportunities present themselves on occasion like when the buyer tax credit went into effect. What has been your experience on the market evolving and how have you met that challenge?

KRISTAN: I think part of keeping up with market evolution is that your business also evolves. Some of your perspective comes from being at a new place in your business because you grow as your business matures. I think sometimes people forget the need to continue some of the basic principles and fundamentals that are simple about this business but that still create immediate results. Those should never go away and should always be part of your plan. For example, when we launched our flagship website with your company in 2005-2006, 60% of our sales were first time homebuyers. Now that has evolved and while we still have a lot of first time homebuyers we also have a lot of move up buyers as well. After you have been in the business for 30 years, and operated with a team for more than 15 years, a lot of the clients we originally had are now moving up and so the demographic of that buyer has not changed that much. Expanding into Anchorage brought in a whole different mix of buyers and sellers apart from Wasilla. I think that the mix of buyers and sellers is not only a function of the market but it may also be a function of interest rates, incentive programs by government and state, as well as other outside forces.

TRICIA: I love what you said about the move up market because, going back to the notes I have from when we first created your Interfusion Marketing roadmap, you had said back then, "Tricia if I could hone in on and improve our transactions and market share in the move up market we would never see the major fluctuations," and you did just that! So for you to say that, is powerful!

KRISTAN: Also the real estate business in general has evolved and me with it! Moving forward, I think we are going to see more expansion teams and expansion markets and they are really going to be a game changer. The company I happen to be with focuses on teams at a very high level. I think now there is a new evolution of that strategy as well. So you're going to be seeing what feels like franchising your own personal brand. I see this as a huge opportunity for real estate agents replicating the basic model they developed, not only the prospecting side of the business, but now how they expand into other markets either close by or even in another state. I think the questions will be, What does that look like? How do you do carry that brand forward? How can you use the core business strengths you already have to leverage expanded business in other locations? The Internet gives us the ability to drive traffic in our favor and it has become the tool that really allows us to evolve and expand which really wasn't possible before the Internet.

TRICIA: That's really interesting because in this book I share the need for core fundamentals such as you are referencing. It's like your DNA, everyone has their own DNA(different hair, different eyes) but they still have basic aspects that are the same. This is also true for business. With that in mind, how does branding become part of that overall business model as you expand markets?

KRISTAN: If you want to gain market share on a long term basis in any location, branding is very important. But before you can think about expanding, you must leverage that brand within your home base that you already know. Once you conquer that, you can then simply take that knowledge into a new area. The home location for me is Wasilla, Alaska, and the core fundamentals of the business that I have implemented are always going to be in that home base, and those are the reason you can expand your business and market into other areas. For me, expanding into Anchorage was the best move I made because some of what I was already doing was bleeding into the Anchorage area making it a lot less difficult to turn on that Internet lead generation "spigot". Once you've got the systems, tools and people in place especially on the administrative side, the big thing becomes finding the who; the person that's going to deliver your value proposition to the public to entice them to do business in another area. That's why you and I are working on a lead generation site for Anchorage. Is that absolutely necessary? No. Could you and I find out a way to generate leads in another way? Probably so, because we have done similar things in the past, through stealth sites and such. But if you want long term name recognition and want to develop a presence and a brand then it is important to build a lead generating site. I don't think it's either/or, although you probably could create business with just one of them, but if you have both then it's obviously faster and more long lasting.

TRICIA: I agree. Thinking about a common storefront we both know, like Target, even though they may have one store in one area and people may drive twenty to thirty minutes to go to that store location they will do a lot more business if they open up a store closer to those customers by reaching into another geographic demographic. You and I have both had several different ideas and approaches with calls to action and such, could you share some of the channels you use to generate leads and why you use those?

KRISTAN: When we first started working together I had stealth ads in our local paper that weren't branded to me but they did assist in driving traffic to us at that time. We've used that for seven years now and only now, at the end of this year, we are going to stop using that avenue because there is so little we can gain from it anymore with all the new things we can do online. We do it so differently because, in Alaska particularly, we have the most computers per household of anywhere in the country, so the Internet has taken over the way people gain knowledge and research. We use the Internet to generate leads as opposed to the newspaper now.

Right before our call I was in a strategic meeting about what one thing we can do in the next eighty days that will generate the business we want in order to hit the goal we made at the beginning of the year. If you're trying to create something short term, meaning to get results now, then it comes down to the basic fundamental that anyone who has ever been successful at real estate did at one point in time, and that is picking up the phone and actually calling people. The interesting part is the people who we will call are the people who have signed up for a free giveaway and other things they can sign up for through our sites online. Even though we talk about the "one thing" we could do for the next 80 days, business people have to know there can't be just one strategy that controls your whole dynamic. It depends on the goal, whether long term or short term, and once again you can't do either/or, you have to do both.

We used to do all of our giveaways through postcards but you and I recently decided the best way for us to kick off our newest flagship site was to change from postcards to online signups. So we delivered our message via Internet and email. What that's done over time has kept us in really close contact with our clients but also allows us to maintain the best contact information and it drives that long term repeat and referral business, which to us is anywhere between 68% and 73%. That's a very large number. This was made possible by staying engaged with our clients through all of our different online programs and community programs that are acknowledged and rewarded by our website.

TRICIA: That's Interfusion in practice; instead of doing just one thing, like tweeting, you bring all of these various aspects together which give larger results and funnel into building more business down the road. What would be your recommendation to people who may want to try out giveaways in terms of how many giveaways and how often?

KRISTAN: You have to deliver the invitation for them to sign up for about six weeks in order to capture the excitement. So we do the giveaway five to six times a year. We send a series of emails letting them know to sign up and advertise the giveaway for about six weeks. Once we have the drawing, we have them come into the office and we take their picture and put it up all over the Internet on our sites and other avenues so that it interfuses with everything. Then when the buyer agents call, they will use the photos of the winners from the last giveaway to leverage people into signing up for the next giveaway. They lead that conversation into allowing the client to help you find more business. Most won't necessarily be all that helpful the first time you call but after a few months of calling they will help you because you have helped them for so long. Persistence is very important.

TRICIA: What are some of the things you are doing to generate seller leads, which is your niche market, right now, like the newer radio ads you've started doing?

KRISTAN: Well I had never done radio in the past because our very small market of Wasilla doesn't associate as well with radio but once we expanded into Anchorage it was obvious that we should use radio ads to have more reach. There is definitely a call to action in our radio ad. It talks about how quickly things are selling on the market and how our clients will have more money as opposed to selling fast. It's a very specific call to action that states 'fast is good but more money is better', which drives them to our seller site of www.AlaskaHomeSellingInfo.com. The interesting part was that the message was targeted for Anchorage but we have also received more listings in Wasilla as a result of the radio coverage and that is new listings we wouldn't have received otherwise. In the first week we ran the advertisement we also had a $600,000 listing in Anchorage and that client also became a buyer for us. When you've got the right message delivered in the right way, you will have some immediate results. Radio for us costs $2,000 a month, and for that we have two ads running in the morning and two in the afternoon during worker commute times. So going into radio created for us, specific expanded business.

TRICIA: I remember when your site first launched you asked me if we had any content that would tell why the site is so powerful for sellers to use. And even though I didn't have anything, we put some thought into it and reworked your seller presentation. That actually inspired me to come up with the seller FSBO toolkit. How do you see that working as you recruit team members that aren't as strong as you yet, because they are learning and on the way up? How important do you think it is that they have books that they can email or drop off and use as a way to bond with the client?

KRISTAN: I think that's incredibly important to have that kind of tool because, as we both know, show versus tell is what works. It is much more powerful to be able to show someone a visual and put it in front of them. I think it's even more important when you are developing team members who, like you said, may not have the highly developed scripts and dialogue skills yet. Having those tools will help them assist our clients to visibly see why our value proposition is so powerful.

TRICIA: If someone were to get started in understanding the audience they wanted to attract and decide the target market they want to work with, what are three things that you could share as to how they might go about it and make sure they do it right?

KRISTAN: They have to begin with the end in mind because there are a ton of different ways to attract business. I think the biggest mistake people make is to try and do all of them as opposed to doing only a few and sticking to them. Are you, for instance, going to use the phone and call prospects or are you going to be more equity based and knock on doors and do open houses? You have to know if you're going to do something like that or do direct marketing. I think for most people getting started, the prospecting base is where they should begin and then enhance it with marketing to build their brand. It is important to understand that success is not simultaneous it's sequential. You've got to take one aspect and do that well at a really high level. If you think about our website, what we started with and what it is today, there's no way we could have built it to what it is today at that point in time because it is sequential. We started small and have added to it as we've gone along. We evolve the website as we gain success in certain lanes of business so it's ever changing. We've said "now we want to move into Anchorage so what will that look like" and we did what I would call a "soft-launch" with those ideas. Once we got our foot in the door, and the right person to deliver the value proposition, then we added radio and now we have a full website specific to Anchorage. You have to know where you are trying to go and what works best with you personally. You can't be everything for everybody and shouldn't try. Just decide what you want to go after and focus on that thing until you have a high level of success. Then, after you've gotten that initial success, add to it, and continue to add more and more. We didn't try to build Rome in a day; we have continually been progressing consistently toward where we are today.

TRICIA: Its very interesting that you mentioned these things because they are a huge part of what I put into this book, and it is so great that you are reinforcing these ideas because some Realtors will say, "give me a site like Kristan Cole" and I have to tell them you don't just do that, you have to roadmap and strategize first and then build. For instance, just because one agent tweets doesn't mean you may have to. You may find success in another avenue. I love to see that you are practicing these same ideas still because that's really what I want the outcome of this book to be; for business people to get these basic principles and then commit to building their own version of success.

Dr. Adam Shapiro

Partner
Foot and Ankle Associates
www.FootAndAnkleAssociates.com

Dr. Shapiro shared with us how niche marketing can serve as a great business strategy. When I interviewed him and discussed his mission of how he serves his patients this is what he shared with me.

TRICIA: As I was preparing for this interview it made me think about how you could have chosen to work in an Orthopedic practice but instead you made the conscious decision to go into the niche of a foot and ankle practice. What drove you into this specialty?

DR. SHAPIRO: I was Premed at the time and had worked with foot surgeons in Atlanta and Emory. I was interested in what they were doing and I knew "this is it". I am also a runner and I like to fix things. I guess that was my introduction into this field. I saw what they were doing and I was interested in it.

TRICIA: From your experience, how important do you think it is to specialize in a practice?

DR. SHAPIRO: In medicine, and every business in general, I think it's very important. The more specialized you are the better off you will be. Nowadays it's pretty hard to find someone who has a general practice that can cover everything.

TRICIA: How has specialization been a catalyst in building your business?

DR. SHAPIRO: The best referral is word of mouth, obviously, but we do get a lot of physician referrals, too, which is a key part of our practice. They recognize us as experts in this area so we come to mind first.

TRICIA: As one of your patients, one of the things you did is educate me on what shoes to buy and how to incorporate certain exercises that would make my foot better. How do you stay dialed in with so many different patients, each with different needs?

DR. SHAPIRO: To me it's almost like a sixth sense. I have treated almost 40,000 patients. Sometimes I can pick up on things that are subtle and aren't necessarily verbal cues. I also like to teach, and people like to know what's going on, so I think if you can help someone understand what the problem is, you are going to be a better partner. Anyone's result is fifty percent me and fifty percent them.

TRICIA: I remember on our second appointment, you said I should have an MRI because the X-ray was unable to show everything like an MRI. You said you couldn't do any deeper without a roadmap to work from. You didn't know my book was on how to create a roadmap to get from point A to point B in your business! I went back and told my husband that you used my method and mindset. That it was a wonderful moment and you were right. The stress fracture showed up on the MRI but it was so small that the X-ray was unable to show it.

DR. SHAPIRO: That is key in finding the right path. Sometimes you need to take an overview and then do an analysis to go deeper into a situation to see how to proceed next.

TRICIA: That is exactly the point I make to businesses. You must have a roadmap and then go deeper with your analysis to really understand your business. One thing that I love about your business, is that your website really practices what I call the five second rule. It has specific buttons right on the homepage to get to the information that people need right away like Ankle, Heel and Diabetic needs. Did you and your team really think through that process? How much did you put into it?

DR. SHAPIRO: We did. We looked at what our patients ask us about most frequently and then made sections on the website to specifically answer those questions. We also have a blog section that talks about special services, treatments or conditions. For example, one of our doctors performs special treatments so there are people who come from all over the state, or other states, because they read it on the blog. We have a lot of that information in there for people to be aware and gain knowledge before they come in for an appointment.

TRICIA: If you could offer an entrepreneur that was looking to specialize some advice, what would it be?

DR. SHAPIRO: Sometimes the best markets are the ones that are the most frequently overlooked. I would tell them sometimes you catch the biggest fish in the smallest pond. If you want to be successful find a niche. Don't fish in Lake Norman, find yourself a small pond. I know it sounds sexier to say you're a Neurosurgeon than a podiatrist, but we are pretty specialized and we never run out of patients. If you want to be successful, you have to do that.

TRICIA: That's a strong point: be true to who you are. That's wonderful advice!

Young Team Realtors

Keller Williams Realty Greater Cleveland
Cleveland, OH
www.YoungTeamRealtors.com

In Section II of the book we talked about how to build an unstoppable brand in your market. When I sat down with Jeff to discuss his brand he was also open to sharing how Interfusion Marketing influences all their success including brand, web strategy, social media and search engine marketing.

TRICIA: From your perspective, how important a roll has having a brand played in your overall business?

JEFF: Amazingly important. In fact, it is probably the one thing, except for lead generation, that makes an impact. We all have to lead generate but our brand is probably the one thing that is most responsible for our success. To the point that, even though I have lived in this community all of my life, people I have known for many years instead of saying "Hi Jeff" when they see me they say, "Hi Young Team". That's how connected we are to our brand.

TRICIA: That's awesome. You have a unique brand that showcases, I think, a lot of your personality. Can you think back and share how you initially developed that brand? Why did you choose the heart and what does it symbolize? How did that become the message?

JEFF: Well, it started out when Terry was an individual agent. And one of the things that I admired about her as a real estate professional, compared to many of the other agents I knew, was she always, always put the client first. It was never about the commission. It was never about the deal. It was about the client and their needs.

She had this genuine love of serving clients in the capacity of real estate. To that end, she is a naturally smiley person and she likes people. People gravitate to her. So, the heart just became a natural symbol of all of that. When you started coaching us, we all knew we both were very outgoing. We like people. We are inquisitive. We are curious and so we're constantly asking questions to learn about people and that personality, that inquisitiveness, ties into the love of real estate and the love of what we do, which is help people achieve their goals. So that is how that evolved.

TRICIA: I have a section in the book that talks about discovering your uniqueness and how that plays into your brand. I have them answer three questions: 1. What do I stand for? 2. What's our competitive edge? 3. Why does it matter?

You just said that your brand really compliments those messages. If somebody were to put you on the spot and ask you to answer those three questions, what would you say?

JEFF: First of all, many people say it, but we live it. We absolutely put our clients first. We've had clients that have said, "You know what, we've listed our house but now we've changed our mind." Some companies would not let you out of your listing agreement. We tell them right up front if for any reason they change their mind that it is no problem. I'd rather we tear up the agreement than have you telling everybody you know that you are stuck with an inflexible Realtor. So, we absolutely live putting the client first. That's number one. Number two, we pretty much do this full time. You know, I play a little golf. We have dogs we walk. We have a few other hobbies; we cook. But we mostly do real estate – it is our passion. I remember a time when I saw agents that seem to do nothing but work and I said, "Gee, they ought to get a life." The fact is when you love what you do it is your life and doesn't seem like work. There is nothing I would rather do. If I get a call from somebody that is coming into town and they want to buy a house, I want to help them find it. It's what we do and what we love doing. And so, that is how the brand, the heart, ties into who and what we are. The last little piece of that is when Terry and I started working together our value proposition was that as a husband/wife team we felt that many of our clients, who are married couples, appreciated that approach. Often one spouse would relate to Terry and one would relate to me. We felt that brought some diversity and added to our complexity and level of service we could provide.

TRICIA: One thing that I'm really hoping that this book gives is for people to really dial in to being unique and also be comfortable with defining what type of person they want to attract into their business and their life.

On your website the one thing that you guys have done is to showcase the market areas that you have serviced in Cleveland and then have featured communities and neighborhoods. How do you feel that has worked as far as creating an impact and generating leads?

JEFF: When we get a listing I always ask our new seller, "Why did you decide to hire us?" And many of them have said, "Your website". One of our value propositions on the listing appointment is that we are already marketing your community even before you have hired us to market your house. That is because of the community feature on the website. We direct them to the website where they see, for example, that if they live in Beachwood we are already marketing Beachwood. The buying population that is looking for Beachwood is just waiting for their house to be listed; they are already looking at Beachwood on our website.

TRICIA: How do you go about searching out new communities or an additional market you want to add on to your site?

JEFF: It's really pretty simple. Cleveland has a river running through the center of it and it's on a lake so basically the city is divided into east and west. We live on the east side. We work on the east side. Although we have served some people on the west side very successfully, our main focus is on the east side. There is a well-defined group of suburbs that are the areas we serve and focus on so those are the areas that we feature. Our market is pretty well defined and our website is also pretty well defined. From that perspective, we keep doing what we do. We focus on improving on it.

TRICIA: Now, if I were a business person and wanted to understand and research my market what advice would you give?

JEFF: Well, I'd say talk to Tricia Andreassen! She'll tell you exactly what you need. That's a bit of a cop out and not really answering your question. You know we relied very heavily on your guidance but clearly your brand and your identity is your hub. We know that people go to websites to look for listings so I would certainly market listings before communities. While it is important to have a page that tells about you, again, people are searching for listings whether they are buyers or sellers. If they are a buyer they want to see your listings to see what is available. And if they are a seller they want to see what you are listing to see if you are a fit for marketing their home. So I would say: home page first, listings second, third clearly you have to have some identity and some value proposition. After that, I would add things like communities and the other lead capture elements.

TRICIA: You are also using tools like your blog and YouTube as well as elements of social media. How did you gravitate to that because it wasn't originally your strength? Do you have any insight?

JEFF: Ryan, on our team, is connected to a whole different generation and those are things they just use automatically. One thing he has done is create a Young Team TV which is a video link on the face of our website. Instead of a standard 360 panorama virtual tour of one of our listings, Ryan will do a video clip which he also can post on YouTube. This will feature more of the special points of that particular listing. If you have a house with an amazing kitchen, he will focus on that kitchen and the dinner parties you can throw for friends and family. He focuses on the feature and the lifestyle. That has been very powerful because we have sold many of our listings simply because somebody landed on Young Team TV and got intrigued by the house. Then they contacted us to find out more about it.

TRICIA: You have also focused on your search engine optimization for a long time and your business consistently ranks on the front page of the search engines. How has that played into your overall business plan?

JEFF: Even though we are not experts at doing the SEO work, I know that because of search engine optimization and because we rank high in the search engines that people are reaching out to us. We're getting the leads and we have mastered the skill of converting those leads. I am absolutely confident, without having studied the subject, that search engine optimization has been huge for us. When we get a listing I ask, "What ultimately caused you to decide to hire us?" When we get leads I always ask them the same question, "How did you find us?" Very often it is the Internet and/or our website. You need to put together a whole package that embraces enough of what's out there so that you actually get the leads and then can follow up on them.

TRICIA: Let's talk a little about some of the unique branding that you have done to set yourself apart even more.

JEFF: Pro Step Marketing designed our whole branding and marketing package which of course included the website, the business cards, stationary, the yard signs and so forth. There is one thing that many people don't do that you have helped us with and it has been huge. That is the Hummer I drive. You designed the wrap and it is so visible that everywhere I go people say, "We see you everywhere." I can say it is second only to the website only because it is local and it is not as broad in scope as the website. It has created such recognition that literally when I go to the supermarket people stop me like they know who I am because they've seen my picture on the side of my Hummer. I know specifically of at least one sale that was generated by that wrap. It was someone we had known a long time ago and didn't stay in touch with but they kept driving by our office and saw the Hummer. Because of it, when she was ready to buy she stopped in and asked for Terry. We of course helped her buy a home. I was driving along on the freeway the other day on the way to the airport to pick up my daughter and my phone rang. I said, "Hello, this is Jeff. How can I help you?" He asked, "Is this the Young Team?" And I said, "Yes it is, how may I help you?" He responded, "I want to list my house." I said "Great we would love to help you. How did you find us?" The man said, "I'm driving right next to you on the freeway." He called me from his cell phone and got my number from the information on the side of the Hummer. It ties back into the comment I made earlier, that the brand is so strong now that people see Terry, Ryan and me as the Young Team and as often as not, they will address us as the Young Team as opposed to our first names.

TRICIA: That's so powerful and makes me feel so happy to know that my company had a hand in that kind of success. I believe it has been seven or eight years ago that we started together and to see you all embrace these ideas and have such explosive success is very affirming.

JEFF: Well, there's one story I will share that is kind of amazing. We were at a business conference, and one of the sponsors had a party where they had a drawing for an IPad. All the cards were in a glass jar and when it was time to draw the card I was standing with someone about ten feet away from the jar. They held the jar up high and reached in to pull out a card. When the card was about half way out of the pile of cards the person next to me said, "You just won". That is how recognizable our business card is.

TRICIA: That's powerful because I think that sometimes people just take the simple way and use a franchise business card, which all look the same. A unique business card is the first way that someone can connect with you and it obviously works!

JEFF: Let me just share one more thought with you because I feel this is important. I could argue that Terry and I live our brand but the only reason I can say that is because the brand that you created for us is completely us. If the brand was not a good fit, it would not be natural. It would be a struggle to actually live and be identified with the brand. But because of your ability to sense who and what we are as people, the brand reflects us and works perfectly. I wear that brand like a custom suit. It feels so natural on me that I don't have to think about it. My daily existence matches and fits with that brand and I think that is why it has been so powerful.

Crystal Carr

Owner
Classic Salon
www.Classic-Salon.com

In Sections I and II we discussed the importance of being your authentic self when building your dream business. Crystal Carr is a young entrepreneur who runs a Salon and Spa in the Lake Wylie, South Carolina area. Crystal shared with me how she is practicing Interfusion Marketing in her business and how she uses the strategies to build her practice for long term success.

TRICIA: You're a relatively young business owner but I wanted to talk to you from the heart about your experiences and pick your brain because you're still evolving. Over the last year, you've seen an opportunity to add additional services like massage. What was your strategy behind that?

CRYSTAL: Most people want more services out of salons. They like going to one place to spend a relaxing day. My clients would mention that idea and I knew that it would be a great fit to have more services for our clients.

TRICIA: There are a couple different things I hear that are tipping points for success. What emotion do you want people to feel when they come and visit your business?

CRYSTAL: For one, I want them to be greeted as if they walked into your home. I want them to come in the door and feel like they belong there. I want them to feel important; I want them to feel like they are in control of the service they are going to receive. A lot of people are scared of haircuts because the stylist doesn't always listen and it can be very stressful. It's important for our clients to feel comfortable and in control of their experience. To feel like it's the best experience they've ever had.

TRICIA: What advice would you give another business owner looking to grow their business?

CRYSTAL: I definitely do recommend focusing on each client as a relationship for the long term. Especially women - we like relationships and many times it's not all about numbers. Of course without numbers you won't be anywhere as a business but relationships are what keep the business going so they are critical. Build clients for life and know your numbers so that you can align with your overall mission.

TRICIA: There is an amazing graphic that's on the wall in your salon that represents your brand. How important do you feel it is to have a strong brand?

CRYSTAL: Branding is very important. I want potential clients to connect to us and know that we are professional in our service offerings. When I was first establishing the brand, I looked at silhouettes because I wanted something simple and something that would stand out. A lot of logos, I feel, are too much. They are too complicated and confusing. I then found a gentleman who painted murals. From that idea, the brand came to life and everything fell into place. Since then, I've been in love with it. It's something very simple but you can make it more exciting with the colors used.

TRICIA: How important do you think it is to have a connection with your client to build your business?

CRYSTAL: Its 100% important. The client actually trusts you and cares about you so they will tell their family and they will speak of you like you are family. They will tell everyone and be excited about telling people very positive things.

TRICIA: How do you find a way to be dialed into what makes your customers tick as far as knowing how to reach out to them in a different way?

CRYSTAL: Just talking to people you can tell what clicks with them by their facial expressions. Something as simple as looking at someone when they are speaking gives you clues to how genuine they are about different things. You pick up on those clues and if you can find something in common, you establish a connection. It might be hard for some people, but I can always speak with someone and find a connection.

TRICIA: Your business message matches who you are. I have a section in the book about that; being your authentic self as a business owner.

CRYSTAL: There are some people I've worked on that I don't care if they ever come back again because we don't match. It's okay to be honest about that. You want to align with the clients that you want to work with. That makes your business fun and successful.

TRICIA: You have done some different marketing and creative things. You do various marketing pushes such as with Groupon, that's sort of unique for your business. Why do you use Groupon and how is it beneficial to your overall business growth?

CRYSTAL: For small businesses, Groupon is the best thing you can ever invest in. Most small businesses like myself can't afford to invest $600 per month for an ad in a newspaper. With Groupon, they hit so many different people and so many different market levels, a lot people are seeing it that otherwise might not see an ad anyway. They also take their money out of whatever they sell so they only make money if you make money. More than likely they will sell a decent amount of Groupons because that is how they make their money. They deal with all the credit cards, and a lot of questions that we don't have to deal with. All of that legwork is on Groupon and not on me. As far as the payments go, if somebody buys your Groupon and comes in, you aren't making anything off of them. The goal internally is get that client to come back and that will make it worth it in the long run. By them coming in we offer them another coupon to come back. This encourages them to come again and by paying us this time instead of Groupon, we are making money. We've actually had quite a few people who used the Groupon because they were shopping for a new salon and once they experienced our great service, they have stayed. Overall it's good simply because most small businesses don't have the money to put forth toward advertising on a regular basis.

Purvis Anderson

Owner
www.SkeeterPro.com

TRICIA: The reason I wanted us to come together is because you've owned a lot of businesses. The main company you own is Anderson Landscaping. In preparing for this book I saw one of your branding pieces which said it was a division of Anderson landscaping, Skeeter Pro. How did you end up carving out this niche specialty business?

PURVIS: I don't think there are many people out there in the world that know you can actually control mosquitoes in an outside environment. A lot of people don't even know the business exist. I think the more people that find out about it the more it will cause the business to take off because there are so many people that want it. It's affordable and it allows you to enjoy your yard. This is something everyone wants. I have literally had people call me and cry on the telephone telling us how happy they are they can go out in their yard. Once I found out the business existed, I did my research on it to find out what it would take to get involved, just to see if it was feasible to make money at. I did it because it made sense.

TRICIA: You saw a need in the market and you created that. I have a section in the book about understanding the market and who you're servicing. Did some of that just sort of seep into your brain because you do work in landscaping and you hear it a lot?

PURVIS: Absolutely, and it hits my own family, my children and my friends so I saw the need. It took me about six to eight months to research it, but I ask people all the time to feel out the price range. It's something I really have to work with the consumers to find the right price. What I've figured out, after being in the business for a little over two and a half seasons now, people will pay to get this done because they need and want it.

TRICIA: Let's talk a little bit about how you advertise. First of all you came up with your brand. It is a really catchy brand with the grass feeling and so forth. Did you have any thoughts as to how that was inspired?

PURVIS: When we first came out with it, we made a list of about sixty names. We wanted the name to relay to people, without them having to read anything, what we are about. A lot of people still don't know that the business exist so it makes them wonder enough to go to the website or look it up. Secondly, we ruled out most of the names because we wanted it to appear in the .com and there aren't a lot of .com's left anymore. We wanted it to be catchy. Due to our southern location Skeeter Pro just seemed to fit us perfectly so that's how we came up with the name.

TRICIA: What are some of the first things you did to get your business out there?

PURVIS: We first made sure we had a website and that is when I called you. We wanted to make sure we had consistency across the board. As far as our advertising goes, we started in the beginning of the mosquito season. It was about June when we got everything rolling so we were already behind the eight ball and we had a small budget when we first began. My theory was, the more I could put into advertising the more I would make. Our business is seasonal so if I can get you to sign up this year I may have your business for the next twenty years. We went out and hit everything we could, real estate signs, flyers, we signed up on Groupon and Living Social, and we bought ads in the local newspapers. We wanted to start local because we didn't want to drive to far in our inexpensive business because we can't charge more for distance. We had to build an area and saturate it. We went everywhere and we even got a truck wrapped to advertise our business in different places. We go out of our way to park it in different areas for the advertisement. It requires time but it is what we felt we needed to do to get our name out there. It works because people would call us and some would ask "What is it?" We thought that's what would happen but we weren't sure. People will read the big print but they don't really read the fine print. They will see the phone number and then you can tell them everything they need to know. We also came up with a low initial rate the first time just to get them to try the product. After that they are hooked and they will buy the product because it works. The internet site helps a lot too. We get a lot of hits on the internet. It has everything you could possibly need about our business and all of our contact info. The more people we can talk to the better off we are. We can sell our product ten times faster on the phone over email.

TRICIA: So when a lead comes in you are a big believer in picking up the phone and calling them right away.

PURVIS: Immediately! The longer you wait to call them the less chance you have of getting the customer. They are impacted by the speedy response. They are often shocked when I call and by then they are already hooked because of your speedy response. In this industry that's very important. Even if they don't answer our speedy response I leave a detailed message telling them when I will call them back and that gives them one more chance, but if I don't get them on the first day, my percentage is cut in half.

TRICIA: You are naturally an entrepreneur, no matter what business it is. What would be three things you would advise someone in doing if they were starting their own business.

PURVIS: The first one is you have to do your research and you have to have a game plan. It's really important that you know exactly what you're going to be doing and exactly how you're going to do it. The second is you have to have a way of marketing that business within your budget. You will have a little business but not the exposure you want without the marketing. You've got to have enough business to get started and get your name out there or it will never happen. The third most important thing is you have to have enough time to be dedicated to make it work. I've seen a lot of people, and even done it myself, start something that was a good idea and let it fall off. Most people start business as a side note. Almost no one does it as a fulltime thing. You have to have enough time to be dedicated to it to make it work because it requires a lot of time on top of the basic eight to ten work hours. Calling people back, searching the internet, and other things for your business takes a lot of extra time. You won't be able to do it as another part time job usually. It may start that way but it will quickly turn into a full time project business.

TRICIA: Let's say you have a company that has been in the service industry business, where they're acquiring clients but they offer a service, not products. They have been in the market for a couple years and they are struggling and wanting to kick up business. What advice would you have for them to turn on that lead faucet?

PURVIS: Branding is critical. Your name has to be out there. Your name has to be such that people know what you're all about. If you see something and don't know what it is, it may be something you can use, but you don't know it so you don't use it. You have to have some sort of incentive program for using your service. We have a referral program and a first time program. Once we have your name we do practice a follow up campaign. I get way more that sign up because they thought about it last year, talked to people, and decided to do it this year. With the flyers we pass out, the email marketing follow up, the mailers we put out, our name is always out there. If you can keep your name out there, even if people passed it up the first time, somewhere down the road it will come back to you.

TRICIA: Thanks for sharing your insights. I am sure this will inspire many!

PURVIS: My pleasure Tricia!

Jeanette Holland

Holland Shepard Group
Realty World First Coast Realty
Beaufort, NC
www.HollandGroupRealEstate.com
www.CarteretCountyHomeSellingGuide.com

Jeanette has been one of my long term coaching clients and it was a pleasure to talk with her about the strategies she has put into place for her business. As a successful Realtor in the coastal areas of North Carolina, she continues to integrate different marketing strategies into her business like advanced web marketing tools and social media.

TRICIA: It's great that we are here together and able to collaborate and talk through how you're doing things in your market. How has your market evolved over the last few years, and how are you staying up on those changes?

JEANETTE: The market went through such a dramatic reversal after we finished with the feeding frenzy of 2005-06. It shocked so many people to the core. The agents that got into the market when all you had to do was pick up the phone, the ones who didn't have the training or the core elements to sustain themselves, were the first to go. I think all of us got a little lazy because it was so easy for awhile and we forgot what our basics even were. We forgot about the things that needed to be done in order to maintain your business. I think the biggest change that we saw was a reevaluation of how we were doing business, why we were doing business and if we wanted to continue doing business. I definitely had to look at all those things and you and I had a discussion about that. We decided we needed to go back to the basics. We went back to the website to see what the clients were doing, we went back to our daily functions to see what we were doing, and then we refined and changed what needed to be changed. We continued the things that were working, but in a more efficient manner. Your roadmap has been a huge help with that.

TRICIA: You've been in your niche of real estate for more than 30 years. How has consumer behavior evolved for people buying in your market? How have they changed the way they are getting information?

JEANETTE: We haven't seen a whole lot of people moving up because people have been trying so hard to hold on to what they have, they weren't thinking of moving up. The people that are looking to come into this area are also very savvy. They already know the market. They don't come to us to find out what the market is. They have already done their research. They come to use to look at properties. They know what the sellers paid for it and they generally get a lot of information about the properties they are looking into. Those of us that have been around for a while have had a lot of adjustments to make because that is very different than when I first started in real estate. The market and the business in general have evolved because of the Internet and social media.

TRICIA: What are some things you are doing to try to put yourself in their sights?

JEANETTE: In our strategy and coaching sessions you and I talk about how social media is evolving and the use of smart phones is constantly pushing the technical aspect of the business. We are always evaluating how we can integrate all of these items so it can progress as quickly and correctly as possible. Facebook, Twitter, websites, the list goes on. Quite frankly I rely on you for a great portion of this because you have your finger on the pulse of all of this integration. My business is to list and sell real estate; I don't want to spend a lot of time trying to learn all of these processes. They are all tools that we need to use, and need to know how to use, but I just want things to work and get our message out.

TRICIA: That's why I felt so compelled to write this book. Even at one in the morning I'm constantly trying to make it better so I appreciate the acknowledgement. That's why I use the word Interfusion Marketing because we have to be very clear about the type of person we are trying to connect to. It's much like fishing in that we have to adjust our bait to catch the right fish. That's really what Interfusion is. Interfusion is knowing and understanding your market and each individual in that market. With that, you are shifting in your business expansion. You now have a property management division. Six to eight years ago that wasn't even on the radar. Why did you do that, and how important is it for a broker, or realtor, to look into taking over new involvements like your property management.

JEANETTE: It's all about service. That has been the one thing at the core of my career from day one. You have to give good service to your clients and customers. I've had clients who would buy in our area but would want to rent their property out while they were not using it. I didn't have that ability, so I would refer them to another company. I constantly had to stay on top of communication with the client because they were dealing and communicating with a competitor. Because of this, I did lose some clients and I realized why it was bad for me.

I decided that if it was my client, and they wanted to rent out their property I would do it for them simply because they were my client. I would not advertise or solicit this because it's not the business I wanted to attract. The good thing was that I was able to have the best in my property management division. I had good properties that I knew because I had sold them. I had to establish the same core values in the property management division that were in the real estate sales division. That's to maintain contact with your clients, get them their funds on a timely basis, and take care of their property. Once we did this, we were able to get the foundation of that business going.

After that, I started getting calls from people that knew we were managing properties for some of our clients and wanted us to do that for them as well. I had to determine whether we wanted to expand into that business or not. We decided to, but on a very selective basis. We avoid rundown properties and we interview the property owners, then we go look at the property. If we feel like it will be too much work and we won't be able to give them the service they deserve, then we turn it down. We have been very fortunate in this business because we are very selective.

TRICIA: I have a section in this book about getting comfortable with who you want to work with and what business you want to attract, and that's what you're doing. Instead of being very general with your property management division and taking anyone, you are very clear on whom you want to work with and what type of person will be a candidate. I think this is very important. You are a very forward thinking person and you and I have been collaborating on changing some sections of your website; adding new target markets and going deeper. What are some things that compelled you to expand and how do you go about looking at what markets you might want to have more dominance in?

JEANETTE: One thing we did was analyze where our business was coming from. We looked at the different markets and tried to do as much analysis of those markets as we could. We asked ourselves some questions before we decided which direction we wanted to go. Questions like: Do we want to continue to deal with the type of property we are dealing with right now? Do we want to grow our business by increasing the average sale price of our listings?

You analyze your markets and determine what you can do to increase your transaction value. We decided to go after some markets that had higher values. We also wanted to expand our vision and horizon, in that, we were being perceived as a historic company for only a small area because that's where we've done the most business. We wanted to change that and be perceived as the business that will work with you all along the Crystal Coast, not just in a very limited area.

TRICIA: You have a section on your site to really compliment that. How important do you think it is to include buttons on your site that prove you know those markets?

JEANETTE: It's vital! If you have someone coming to your website looking for a home in one area and you don't have that area on your site then they are going to leave your site. This was an epiphany for me when I had a client call and tell me that the area he was selling in was not on my site. He wanted to know how anyone would know his house was available. That's when we decided to go after these targeted markets and areas that would have the best growth potential. We felt this is where we need to establish ourselves.

TRICIA: Some people think they will be better off if they don't target any specific areas within their site for the same reason you noted. What would you say to someone like this who thinks they don't want any specialty sections on their site at all?

JEANETTE: You will lose a lot of business. I really like the part of our site now where, if you move your cursor over certain areas, you get a drop down menu that has neighborhoods and cities within that area. This really engages the potential client because it makes them want to go deeper into the site. You don't want them to just hover around the surface because you can't secure a lead from that. I don't want a very busy site, but I want it to be something that will make the person searching for a home stay on the site.

TRICIA: I call it the five second rule. In five seconds the potential lead has to find something they are looking for. That's what's going to create the stickiness and cause them to bookmark your site and come back to it later. Let's talk about your branding. You have an amazing brand, you're very well known in your market, but your branding is evolving a bit. Share how you're brand is evolving at this stage in your growth.

JEANETTE: We worked really hard when we first established the logo, design, colors, and everything else. It has been very successful. People will see our brand and they don't even read it anymore, they just recognize it. No matter where it is, they recognize it, and it's an automatic response. I don't want that to get stale. I want to spice it up a bit to cause them to notice a change and create curiosity. The major thing we are doing right now is bringing on some young, and very excited, new blood. It has put a spring in my step because when you are dealing with young people, they think differently which is invigorating. We are getting energy, enthusiasm, and an excitement that's going to carry over to our brand.

TRICIA: You use a moving truck in your market. How are you using that moving truck and what influence does that have in your market place?

JEANETTE: The truck sits out on the highway when it's not being used, so it's the biggest billboard you could have, and I get all sorts of comments from people who have seen the truck. We obviously allow the clients to use the truck when they are moving. I have a couple who has put their house on the market and they are going to relocate to Virginia to be closer to their children and they were talking about renting a trailer to move some items. I told them about the truck and offered it for them to use. They didn't know they could use it and were so excited. When they took it to Virginia they had people asking them about the truck and our business and they told them, "That's my real estate agent." That kind of endorsement is priceless. Word gets around, and I have had people call and tell me they want to list their house, but only if they can use our truck. Of course I do have to ask where they are taking it because I don't want it going to California, but it's a great service for them. We also lend it to other places and groups such as charities. The boys and girls club use it several times a year, as does the local museum, and other local community events and non-profit organizations and it's always good to have your brand associated with those things.

TRICIA: What I love hearing is that this really is Interfusion Marketing in practice. You use a different tool to build business and get your message out. You're using a different advertising channel, like Kristan Cole and her radio ad, or Shane White and his tailgates, this moving truck is your unique item. These marketing techniques are all different, but they all begin with the end in mind as to how you can build your brand, how you can build business and generate leads, and how it supports your mission statement. In regards to different channels, like YouTube, Facebook, LinkedIn, Craigslist, and others, what are some things you feel are non-negotiable when it comes to advertising and marketing?

JEANETTE: Right now the first thing is the website. You can't stay in this business and succeed without a good one. It goes back to when I was tracking where our dollars were coming from. We had been advertising in the *News and Observer* for years, so when I started tracking I discovered we did not make one sale from that advertising. If you don't track what you are doing and don't know where your numbers are coming from, you are losing. I know a majority of my business comes from the Internet or an Internet related activity.

TRICIA: This is why it's important to have those targeted sections on your website to attract those leads and give them something of value.

JEANETTE: That's right!

TRICIA: If you were talking to a new business owner who had been in business less than a year, and they really want to build their business for long term success, what three pieces of advice you would give them?

JEANETTE: The first would be to develop a contact management system. If you do not have the ability to track your clients and leads, and keep up with it, you will lose a lot of business. Fill that contact management system with people who love and trust you. Then ask them to call people on your behalf and recommend you to those people. You also need an Internet presence. You have to have something that will make people want to contact with you because of what they see on the Internet; that really evolves into a personal website. You have to stay in contact. You call people and send them notes, which is hard to do, but it's part of the basics. It's part of what you need to do in order to succeed, and it has to be consistent. You can't do it for a few weeks and then stop for a few weeks. You have to be persistent and consistent.

Linda Hall

Century 21 First Choice
Ranked In Top 100 Century 21National
#1 South Carolina and North Georgia
2013 Technology Agent of the Year Award
Real Estate Tribal Group Speaker
www.LindaHall.com
www.YourGuideToHomeSelling.com

As Linda's strategic marketing coach for several years it was exciting to sit back and reflect on the strategies we put together and how her business is continually growing. In Section III we focused on how important it is to have a website that connects to your target audience while providing useful information that is unique from your competition.

TRICIA: I remember the day I had been referred to you. Do you remember that day?

LINDA: Yes I do! I've had a website since the late 90's. I had hired someone locally and paid them $1,500 and they put up a website with no real marketing but I was happy because I had a website. Several years passed. More and more Realtors were becoming involved on the web and Internet. One day I woke up and said "Okay, I have a website, now what do I do with it?" So I had a talk with Stormy, my Realtor.com representative. I told her, "I need to find somebody who can coach me, train me, and design for me, because the Internet is taking over." That was the day I threw up my hands and accepted the fact that I am a real estate specialist, not an Internet specialist, and then you came to save the day!

TRICIA: I remember the day you said you felt like it was a maze. Do you still feel that way? Do you still feel that the Internet and other avenues are a maze for people to try to figure out what to do with?

LINDA: I think it is twenty times bigger than it was when we started. In the home market place, when we began, there were very few people who really had a living website. Today there are thousands and thousands of Realtor websites. I believe that it definitely feels like a maze for an agent to try and put a website together. You've coached me for years and you know that some days it still feels like a maze even for me, because there are numerous things that continue to pop up every day. Because of this, I really do feel like the Internet and other avenues can feel like a maze for people, new and experienced.

TRICIA: I have to go back to what you said about the website being a living thing because I mention in my book that people need to treat their website like a living breathing entity. If you think about your relationship with friends and family and notice how they evolve, we have to make sure that our website and our relationship with that website keeps that same evolutionary progression. How important do you think it is to treat your website like it is never halted and always progressing?

LINDA: I think it's very important. If you look at the stats today you will notice that the Internet makes up a major part of business traffic. Just last year I broke down my total sales in a six month time frame from January – June and 50% of my closed business came from my website. This is the top generating factor for traffic and business revenue for me. I think it is very important that you watch and maintain your website. You cannot just allow it to sit idle, you have to be involved in it and I think that is something that is overlooked by many realtors today. They put their website up and they never keep an eye on it. I'm constantly watching my website, because so much of my business depends on Internet leads.

TRICIA: There are many business owners or salespeople that are running their own business and are afraid to niche market. Instead, they want to work a huge area. The other day I had a business owner that wanted to service an entire metro area of 1.8 million people but didn't have the staff or resources to do it. What would you say to that?

LINDA: I would say, "Are you crazy!" You can't be all things to all people. To try and market to that type of population, in my opinion, would be worthless. You know I have always marketed to a geographic target market. I am really good at what I do in my market. I've made a fantastic living in that market. Have we expanded? Definitely! We look every year to possibly expand out of where we are, but we look at that expansion in neighborhoods, and niche markets within the larger target.

TRICIA: One of the things that you continually do, and you and I collaborate on frequently, is really knowing and understanding your audience. Understanding what makes them tick. Having things in your site and marketing to entice them to do business with you. Things like a seller Ebook or a buyer Ebook. How important, do you think it is to really understand the challenges, desires, or concerns of the people within you niche.

LINDA: You have to know your market. I am a statistical person. I know the age group, I know what my average sale price is, and I know the niche that we work in. It is very important to know the buyers and sellers within your niche.

TRICIA: I love what you are saying about being involved with your market because in several places in the book I talk about how it is absolutely necessary to stay involved with you market and really watch the trends and shifts within the market so you don't get "caught behind the eight ball", so I really agree with what that idea.

LINDA: I continually watch the trends in the market so that we can adapt to that change.

TRICIA: You have a very well established brand, how much do you think that plays into your overall business?

LINDA: I think the biggest thing I've done with my brand is that it is consistent. The brand was designed to be a consistent strategy. It is on everything. The biggest thing

I use when branding is my experience. As it turns out, branding was decent when we started, but today is far more important. *The Wall Street Journal* just came out with a study that experienced Realtors typically, when they are chosen, generate $25,000 more on property. It's that determination and experience with your branding that matters. I've had a billboard, which some people do not believe work, but I'm here to tell you they work, if they are properly branded and are in the immediate area of where you work. I've had a billboard for over fourteen years. It's completely branded; however, it was changed this year to show my support of the humane society by adding the presence of my golden retriever. It's these associations that help get you business and assist your branding with a positive message. The branding evolves and changes the way your business does, you can't just be plain and stay that way.

TRICIA: I believe what you focus on, you find and it expands. It expands because you continually focus on the message that you want to bring to your clients. Let's talk about web strategy. Your website is unique, and this book is on Interfusion Marketing, which is being very clear on your brand, your message, and your niche market. Blending the message through different channels and avenues, such as your billboard, and your Facebook page. It's important, however, to remember that in the beginning you focused on core ideas, like having unique sections on your site and a strong MLS search engine. As a real estate professional how important is it to have a MLS search that's unique, within your site.

LINDA: If you don't have an MLS search that's unique, you might as well not have a site. The first thing people do when people go to a site is search for homes. I see it on the sites and in the statistics; that is what people look for first. Once they get on your site and find the MLS search then they begin to see the other unique qualities. I believe if you are a single agent or a team then it is necessary to have bios on your site that people can read. For instance, a buyer came to our site, read the bios of the buyer agents and read a testimonial of one of our clients. After doing that, he called and asked to have the agent that represented that testimonial. Your site needs to have the best search tool for listing, information about yourself and your team, and another thing I offer on our site is a preferred vendor section that we constantly change, and it's printable. When I'm on a listing appointment I always show the client where to find this section because it is such a big help to them. There are so many more things and you just need to constantly watch and stay in touch with what people are looking at on your site. No matter what industry you service you have to solve the problem for the client and answer the questions that are on their mind non-stop.

TRICIA: That's fantastic advice! How much of an influence do you think it is on your leads to have price ranges within the towns on your website, and neighborhood links so they can see houses in each neighborhood?

LINDA: I think people search by price, and if you don't have the prices then these people are finding far too many listings. Today the consumer is completely different than they were prior to 2007. They stick closer to price ranges and are much more specific when it comes to what price they want. They hear about neighborhoods and then they look up information about them on your site so you need neighborhood links, listings, and pictures within your neighborhood section. People listen to other people because they know they will tell the truth whether it's good or bad. When people transfer from other states they go to the new location and get word of mouth referrals on which neighborhoods they should look for. When you have these neighborhoods and listings with specific prices on your website, then you havea much better chance of securing that lead.

TRICIA: I watch your site all the time and know you generate a lead, on average, every eight hours. You are positioned very well on Google because of the search engine optimization strategy you have in place. How important do you think this is to your overall strategy and how do you think it is affecting your business?

LINDA: If you try to build your site specifically around paying for clicks it will gain search engine position but the minute you stop it will fall. Today you may have to do both pay-per-click and SEO to get the site where you want it to be and have it maintain stability.

TRICIA: You have several Ebooks that help your clients with steps in the real estate process. How important do you think it is to have value added items like that available even if the prospects haven't reached out to you yet?

LINDA: It is definitely something of value because it tells you what to do and how to go about the process if you are even thinking about selling and now with the Internet people are remembering a name. For instance LindaHall.com, they remember this name and come to me, and call me when they have those types of questions. Then I converse with the person, arrange CMA's, and give them information that will help them move forward. It's all about reconnecting. You have to have things of value like these Ebooks. They are fairly new to the market and I've wanted them for as long as you've been designing them. We've now started to send out a postcard that has links to our website on the bottom to engage the person who got the card to entice them to check out these items. I actually had someone call me recently and the first thing they said was, "Hey, I got your postcard."

TRICIA: You have several different stealth websites. What is the thought behind that?

LINDA: There are different types of buyers and sellers out there in my market. A conversation with a For Sale By Owner is going to be vastly different than a conversation with a seller facing foreclosure. You strategized with me to help design different websites that relate to that specific target market. For example, my website www.YourGuideToHomeSelling.com is focused on helping folks look at how to sell their home whether it be with a Realtor or on their own. I also have targeted websites to help buyers like www.FortMillNewHomes.com as the new home market is a big part of our real estate inventory. Different websites allow us to cast multiple "nets" out to attract different consumers.

TRICIA: As a final thought, if there were three things that someone absolutely must do to have a workable, solid plan that's going to get them started on the right path, what would those things be?

LINDA: First: design a plan, and decide who you want to be. If you're a first time agent or an experienced agent who has never had a plan. Think about who you are, what you want to be, and design a brand. It could be family oriented, experience oriented, or nearly anything you can think of. Be sure it is consistent and put it on everything you have. This business is an investment related business. It needs some form of investment to be very successful. You do not need a lot of money but you do need something to invest.

Second: You need a website. But this website has to be geared to your market, with something you can present. This is because the very first thing a seller will ask is, "Do you have a website?" But don't just get one. It needs to be well developed and designed which is why it pays off to have someone like Pro Step Marketing to help.

Third: Put every person you meet into a database. The person who merged their team with mine taught me something even after all these years. Everyone will buy a house or list a house, no matter who they are or where they come from. If you come into contact with them they will either buy or sell a house. So the three things you need to be successful in this business are Branding, Internet, and Database. I know Realtors that have been in this business for twenty years that lose so much by not having a database. If you do not have a system to touch base with clients within your program you are losing so many leads and so much revenue.

Shane T. White

Real Estate Tribal Group Speaker
CRS conference panelist
Broker/Owner
RE/MAX Town & Country
Liberty Hill, Texas
www.ShaneTWhiteTeam.com
www.SellingYourHomeGuide.com

Shane White has experienced growth in his market by developing his brand and web strategy that allows him to stand out from the crowd. His practice of Interfusion Marketing continues to evolve and expand.

TRICIA: We were just talking about how there are still fundamental and core things that we have to do in our business beyond just creative marketing. You've done that in the seven years we've worked together. One thing you do, and over the last year it has been your biggest focus, is adapt to the changes in your market place. You see trends and adapt to them appropriately. How do you go about keeping a pulse on the market and adjusting your approach to fit those changes and trends?

SHANE: I think you have to be aware of what is going on in the market and where the market is headed. You have to keep in mind the progress of your business and continue looking forward because even though you do not know for sure what will happen, you have to have goals and predictions of where you see your business going and where you want your business to be. All of this is, however, tied into really knowing and understanding your market.

TRICIA: Speaking of knowing your markets, when you sit down behind the scenes to focus on new markets, what are some of the things you are doing to evaluate which markets to even take into consideration and expand to?

SHANE: We start within proximity of my office because I don't really want to expand to South Austin which is nearly a forty-five mile drive, because it doesn't make sense with the current size of the business. Right now there are still a lot of opportunities that are close to where my office is, and a big eye opener for me was that the core of our business has been rural properties. When I started analyzing where we are taking listings, since we did such great rural business, I noticed that, though we may be driving fifteen to twenty miles to get to those listings, we never looked south of us to move into the more urban areas and neighborhood locations. So the eye opening moment was when I realized that we would drive fifteen to twenty miles to get to these rural listings but we wouldn't go seven miles to list properties in neighborhoods that would sell in thirty days or less. With this being said, we did start expansion in proximity to my office but from there we moved to areas where there would be turnover of properties which is one of the biggest things when you think of expanding and moving out into new areas. You don't want to go into a stale neighborhood and you want to stay away from neighborhoods where builders are still building new homes because they will have incentives and promotions that you won't be able to keep up with as easily. If you stay away from these things and really focus on getting a finished neighborhood that is pretty large, without a lot of inventory, then you can try to penetrate that market. Once you do that you can continue with your onsite marketing, like sold signs, postcards and similar things, that will allow you to capitalize on the fact that the neighborhood has quick turnover because that is key when expanding and growing into these areas. It goes back to studying, knowing, and understanding your market and having a clear idea of where you want to go, because even though those houses were slightly under our normal sell price, I was able to sell those houses in almost half the time it took to sell the rural homes. This balances out and makes about the same amount of money in terms of time invested in the property. That's how we analyzed how and where to expand to gain market share. You want to do that where selling the properties will be easy and it's not too far away from the office.

TRICIA: How important is it to have targeted content in your website with specific pages?

SHANE: This is important for any market that you're trying to go into. You have to look like you're the expert. One of the ways to do that is to create specific pages on your website. That's what we did with Blockhouse Creek. We had a ton of information and links about what was going on in the neighborhood, the HOA site, and we had all kinds of pictures from around the neighborhood. This, as a listing agent or marketer, helps me show how we are experts in your area and we are interested in your market and neighborhood so much so that we've created a marketing section that is personal to your area. Then we can show how easy it is for buyers to find a house. This gives you the ability to show that you are an expert even if you don't have a lot of market share in that particular area. The typical consumer doesn't know how many agents work Blockhouse Creek, and there will still be a few dominate ones that people know just like we are known in Liberty Hill because we have a lot of business and a lot of signs. When you don't have this previous success and market share in the area then you definitely need this type of webpage you can show the client whether they are a potential seller or potential buyer. You can show them firsthand what is going on, what information you have to offer and how you are going to market their property.

In going back to the neighborhood aspect, we were at one point starting to add a neighborhood every week to two weeks because, with the mentality of the buyer, you want your site to have information that they are looking for because it will lead them to stay on your site longer and they will eventually register or ask for additional information. It's a great tool for listings but I also think it's a huge deal for buyers.

TRICIA: I agree, and building a strategy that attracts buyers allows you to have a natural conversation with the sellers to explain how you're attracting buyers. That is expertise that you provide to the seller whereas without you they wouldn't know how to go about getting that exposure, so that is definitely important. In regards to your branding you were talking about how you've had market share but we also have to look at competitors. You have a well-established brand in your market. How important do you think that is to your business practice and fundamentals?

SHANE: I think it's huge! We started off with the RE/MAX brand by itself and my father-in-law had bought the RE/MAX franchise that we own back in 1999. He was just an independent broker back then so he didn't have a way to attract the customers from outside the area. When we bought the company from him in 2003 we started looking forward and knew that at some point in time our market would grow large enough that our RE/MAX brokerage would need to have other agents that are not associated with the team. You and I had this discussion early on when we teamed up with you to do the website and logo. We talked about how even though we were well known in the market place with RE/MAX, I also needed to create a separate brand for my team so that as our RE/MAX brokerage grows, or other RE/MAX agents come out and list properties, our team brand would stand out separately from that. That's where we brainstormed and came up with logos and colors, and thought about how we could co-brand with the RE/MAX brand.

From this branding, people will know your name. They see your signs, your marketing, what you do for the school and they just know you, whether they've met you or not, because you have so much exposure in the market place. I think it's huge because we try to track all the exposure we get. We ask all of our listings how they heard about us which creates the buzz and energy, and people call because they want to work with someone who's active in the market and knows the market. From a branding standpoint I think it's critical that you have the right kind of branding out in the marketplace so people see it constantly.

TRICIA: I've mentioned that in the branding section of the book, and your name specifically, because you are being mindful of who you're attracting. You and I are very close in age and we are established in an industry so I think people are attracted to that kind of solid business persona. You may be at a football event, or the RE/MAX balloon event for your school, and you've done fundraisers so people recognize you and have a positive association even if they don't know you. Consistency is important as is aligning with the audience you are trying to attract. You do very unique things within your market, like the fundraisers, and tailgates, and being out in the community in unique ways. How much of an influence do you think that has on your overall business?

SHANE: I think it has a pretty large impact. We do various events, like high school football tailgates, because high school football is such a big deal in Texas. We even advertise it on Facebook, and it allows us to relate with the community and communicate with them. Even though we don't set those tailgates up where we can push our business onto them, they always ask about the market. Whether the market is good or bad they always ask about it. Not that they plan on doing anything right now but they still want to know. If you own a house, you want to know if the value is going up or going down, and whether you're selling or not. This type of event gives you those opportunities; that tailgate was right in our office parking lot, and even if you didn't stop you still had to notice our office when you drove by. We took the RE/MAX balloon to the school for a science program they do, and that means 500 elementary school kids and their parents are seeing that first thing in the morning, then we end up in the paper and that's free advertising. It's things like that you want to do to give back to the community but there is also the exposure incentive behind it. That's not the only reason we do it of course, because we do also want to give back.

T-shirts is also a big thing we do where we give every faculty member in our school district from the school board members to the cafeteria workers t-shirts, and when people wear those its more advertising for us, but they also get a nice shirt, and it shows that we appreciate our schools. That's a big thing because people move to our area because we have such a great school district. When I give out the shirts to our faculty they think it's such a great thing, but I thank them for creating such a great school system because that affects my business. The things that you're passionate about and support you can take part in and inevitably it helps your business by having a positive impact on your community.

TRICIA: I know we've touched on target marketing and technology but one of the things that keeps coming up for me is how you are connecting with your audience.

You seem to be authentic and know about your market completely. It is important to know who you enjoy working with and who you will naturally make an impact on because there is a stronger connection. Any thoughts on that?

SHANE: It's important for you to work with the people you are already comfortable being around because whatever you enjoy doing with your community will allow you to make connections and opens up a lot of opportunity in that area. Whether it is golf, tennis, or charity work it doesn't matter what you like to do, you are going to get exposure for your business with the activities you are already doing. You have to look at what hobbies you take part in and what sports your children are involved with so you know how you can leverage that to bring in business.

TRICIA: If you were to share three things with an established business that's looking to go to the next level, what would you have them look at to refresh or improve?

SHANE: They must have a clear written business plan with a clear written marketing plan. You have to analyze your business, understand the numbers and understand what it looks like to be in that place in time. Then you have to figure out how you are going to get to the next level which is how the marketing comes into play, whether you go to your past clients or expand to a new market. Number one is to have a clearly written business and marketing plan; that way you have an idea of what to do. Number two is to know your numbers. How much does it cost to run your business? A lot of what we do as agents is look at how much marketing cost we have, but we also have to look at how much each deal costs, and how much it cost to do business in total. This will give you an idea of what you have to make to be sure you are profitable. You have to know total revenue and cost and then also know your profit percentage.

If you are adding anything to your business you need to make sure that any dollar you spend is actually bringing in business to pay for itself. This has to be part of your business plan too, but you have to know the numbers financially. It is very easy to let money slip through your fingers and have nothing to show for it.

The third thing is to be sure the team you have is the right team. You have to be sure you have the right people in the right position to propel your business forward. It may be that you have to hire an additional staff member. You have to be smart because you don't want to be overstaffed but you need to be sure you have the time personally to create the business without spending time on other administrative things. You need to be sure you keep your team in mind when trying to go from one step to the next. I think those are the three important things when it comes to advancing from one place to another.

JR Hearld

Owner
Cabbellas Coffee Shop
www.CabbellasCoffeeShop.com

I remember JR first opening his coffee shop! From the beginning we collaborated on how to create a website that would match the "heartbeat" behind his brand and tell a story. It was also important to show how his coffee shop was unique with photos and more. Here is what he shared with me in the interview.

TRICIA: When you opened your coffee shop what did you want to fulfill in the market?

JR: We wanted a place where local people could come and feel at home. Where they could enjoy a good product at a good price without feeling rushed.

TRICIA: How did you go about creating your brand?

JR: Creating the brand is never ending. Even the emotion of people feeling like they were home came into play. It starts and ends with being consistent with all you're marketing/advertising, keeping logos the same, and sticking with the same colors. We wanted a warm and friendly atmosphere so that is why we chose the warm colors. Our tag line also relates to the emotion behind our service of "Come home to Cabbellas."

TRICIA: How does that carry throughout the inside of your shop?

JR: Our logo and name is sprinkled throughout our store so the warm colors we advertise with on the outside we decided to stay consistent with on the inside as well. One unique thing we did was a mural picture that is on the main wall in our business. That picture is also the main photo on our website. Since we want them to feel at home, I have staged the room with a fireplace, a fish tank that the kids can enjoy, as well as coffee tables and sofas. I want them to enjoy the atmosphere and that is key to our brand.

TRICIA: What emotion do you want people to feel when they visit your shop?

JR: We want people to not want to leave and feel welcome to stay as long as they would like.

TRICIA: How did you go about choosing Denver, NC for your location?

JR: We felt that Denver suited us and our family values. Small and family oriented as to our exact location. It was God inspired.

TRICIA: You have unique pages in your site like a photo gallery, a blog and you feature coupons for web visitors. How important do you feel these elements are?

JR: I can't say enough about the importance of a web presence in today's market. After our website was launched we had people coming in and saying they found out about our business online, especially travelers and people who were new to the area. These elements are a huge factor.

TRICIA: You also rank highly on the search engines and on page one on Google when people are looking for a coffee shop in the area. How has that played a role in your business growth?

JR: Getting found on the web is extremely important. In today's world people are on their mobile and conducting a search possibly from their car and we want to be top of mind for them. If we are not online, we don't exist to those who don't know us yet.

In the beginning, when you helped me develop my strategy, we talked about how to build sections on the geographic areas so that I rank for those specific keywords. My site is constantly being evaluated and I am able to see how people are finding us and what they are typing in to locate us. These tools allow me to stay aware of how to continually make additions to our site so that we rank highly. Right now we are number two on Google for Lake Norman Coffee Shop. It can't get much better than that.

TRICIA: You mentioned to me that your business is always evolving, what did you mean by that and what has transpired?

JR: Our business continues to evolve around the needs and wants of our customers. If you hear something enough times you can't ignore it. For example, if ten customers within two months ask for honey at your creamer station then you should probably put honey at your creamer station. We listen to customer's suggestions on a daily basis. If you listen to your customers, they will tell you what they want and need. That is the key to growing your business.

Holli McCray

KW top 150
Real Trends Top 10 TN Team
The Holli McCray Group
Keller Williams Realty
Knoxville, TN
www.HolliMcCray.com
www.KnoxvilleForeclosureHelp.com

I had a wonderful opportunity to visit with Holli McCray and hear about the success she has experienced in her business since we started working together. Here she shares her views on how following the market and having a strong brand in your niche can fuel your business. Her Interfusion Marketing strategies of blending her web marketing with other media outlets like radio and Facebook have proven to be a great formula for success.

TRICIA: It's great for us to come together. One thing you had said while speaking at a conference was that you have to follow the money in your market, and I think what you meant is that you have to follow trends in your market. Share with me your philosophy and how you continually evolve with your market.

HOLLI: In 2008, the market was tanking and John decided he wanted to go into short sales. I thought for sure he had to be kidding, but he had me look at what was happening in that area. We had markets all around us that were ahead of us and all of them were in the foreclosure alley, so that was bound to head into our area sooner rather than later. We didn't have a great rise and great fall, we had a small rise, small fall, but we still had it. We knew, beyond a shadow of a doubt, that no one in this market would pick up short sales. With all of his experience in banking we really started brainstorming about it and that turned out to be incredible for us.

After we started working short sales, we would get clients referred to us by other agents because they didn't know how to do a short sale. That's when we realized what a strong niche that was, and we started thinking about what our next niche would be because we knew this could not continue forever. We started looking from niche to niche analyzing the market and the data. Once you do that you can see, from a mile away, where you need to be marketing.

TRICIA: You have focused heavily on building your brand in your market. Why did you do that, and what affect has it had on your overall business?

HOLLI: It's been huge! I wanted to do it because I wanted to expand outward. There is a very low barrier of entry into Real Estate. People see the dollar signs and they get a real estate license, but what they don't realize is that you are running a business. With that in mind, we did not want to be lumped in with the other agents that didn't run their office like a business. We wanted the public to know, this is business, we are serious, this is our career, and we are experts. When consumers are swimming in a sea of information, they don't know what is correct. We knew that we really needed a brand and presence in the community. We needed to make it obvious so prospects would seek us out without us having to convince them. We just really needed to stand out, and it's worked beautifully.

TRICIA: When somebody comes to your website, they see a photo of a baseball field. What was the thought process behind choosing that photo?

HOLLI: There were a lot of different thought processes but the long and short of it is that it's not about the money; it's never been about the money. We were very financially challenged when we started this business, but we knew that it would work. The baseball picture helped us focus internally. One of the things that we love is to help kids and one of the dreams that we've had is to do something with that money. My family loves baseball and that picture, to us, really represents the heartbeat of what we are doing, where we are, why we are doing it. It helps put into perspective that it's not about the money; it's about helping the people. The general public probably sees it and wonders why there is a baseball field, but for us it's the best "gas in the tank."

TRICIA: I have a section in my book about passion and motivation and how that's like the sugar of the DNA strand because if you don't have sugar the DNA won't stick together, so I love it when you talk about your passion. Your family loves sports, you're sports people.

HOLLI: We are sports people, John played in college and our son is playing sports now and he loves it.

TRICIA: You were very aware of what fonts you wanted to use. What was that experience like for you? What did you gravitate to and why?

HOLLI: I gravitated to less standard fonts. I wanted more edgy and less traditional. If I had my way, nothing would be traditional. I live in Knoxville which is very traditional so we do stick with that strand a bit.

TRICIA: Now you're using different ways to get the word out. One of the things you do is radio. Share with me how that works and what that looks like. What kind of offers do you put out on the radio and what does that look like?

HOLLI: Radio has been really successful. It's one of those leap of faith things because it's very expensive to do it right. A lot of people who do radio don't do it right but it's been a wonderful way to spread that message to a wide audience, and an audience of our choosing. We know we aren't a match for every client on the planet; no one is. We do know, however, who our message is a match for. The radio has given us a way to reach that audience on a very broad scale. We do offer some incentives on the radio because we want to stand out just like we do on the Internet. One thing that we are awesome at is providing great, no obligation information. Agents for years have been doing the same old thing. Why do we continue to advertise a CMA when no one knows what it is? We offer things people want to know. People want to know what their house it worth now. People want to know how the market is and how it applies to their address. They hear the news and go by what they hear but national news does not necessarily apply to our next door neighbors. We have the ability to drill down and give people excellent data about the market for their address. It's really awesome when you go into a listing appointment, you hear what the seller thinks, sit down with them and show them how this information actually applies to them because they don't really know. Sometimes it's better news than they think so it's really great to be able to go in and give them that information. We sell a very high percentage of the houses we list because we go in with very accurate data. We know what we're doing, we know what it's going to take to sell, we know what the buyers are looking for and we need to keep a pulse on that in order to be successful. This way we can guide sellers as well. We are smart enough now to know what data is relevant and how to get the results people need. We are extremely honest with our clients because there is no reason to inflate a listing price just to put a sign in the yard. That doesn't lead to our mission.

TRICIA: Besides radio, do you do direct mail in your market? If not, what other kinds of advertising do you use?

HOLLI: We do not use direct mail at this point. We do a lot of Internet marketing and SEO behind the scenes. John loves doing that and it works beautifully. The results are definitely there. All of the things we are doing bring us over 700 buyer leads per month for our sellers and we can, if we want, hit a button and generate more. We really know how to do that now, and I think that's a great service to our sellers. We continue to find out where buyers are, and where they are looking, because you obviously have to think like a buyer in order to sell a house. We spend a lot of time pretending to be buyers and acting like buyers to bring the two together. That is pretty much Interfusion Marketing isn't it?

The Seven Laws of an Interfusion Marketing Strategy

You are now ready to put your own Interfusion Marketing strategy to work. You will find that these ideas will apply to your team meetings, your marketing plan, your website navigation, your prospecting, your lead generation, and even your client conversations. But no matter what you do, always base your decisions on your unique DNA and what you want for your business. Here are seven laws which will be the overseeing guidelines for everything you do in your business. Within these guidelines, you can craft unlimited tactics that will set you apart as the leader in your market.

Using your DNA code, you will apply these seven laws to increase your market share and reach new levels of success—your way.

1. Always be thinking forward, planning and innovating.

2. Always have a clear message to reach a specific audience.

3. Always specialize and stay focused on the needs of your target market.

4. Always spread your marketing message everywhere using multiple marketing channels.

5. Always be consistent in your branding and presentation.

6. Always evaluate your market and the evolving trends.

7. Always follow up on every lead and have systems in place to manage those leads and track the results.

When you keep these top of mind you will be successful. Here's to reaching new heights in your business!

(Endnotes)

1. Cell Press (2009, January 16). Brain Mechanisms Of Social Conformity. ScienceDaily. Retrieved September 26, 2013, from www.ScienceDaily.com/releases/2009/01/090114124109.htm

2. National Association of Realtors, 2012 Profile of Home Buyers and Sellers

3. www.Entrepreneur.com/article/175428

4. National Association of Realtors, 2012 Profile of Home Buyers and Sellers

5. The Lead Response Management Study: www.LeadResponseManagement.org/lrm_study

6. Direct Marketing Association, 2012 Channel Preference Survey, UPSP Postal Bulletin 22312 and USPS Mail Moment Survey www.Newsroom.fb.com/Key-Facts

7. The One Thing by Gary Keller

About the Author

Over the last two decades, International Speaker, Business Strategist and Certified Executive Coach Tricia Andreassen has trained and coached thousands of real estate professionals and business owners on how to finally get the results they have always wanted. With an emphasis on creating a powerful partnership and synergy between vision, brand, web strategy, print marketing and all marketing channels including social media, she brings hands-on, cutting edge creative practices that can set you apart from your competitors and get amazing results.

Tricia first started her love for business at the age of 19 while working her way through college and on a fast track for success was managing a real estate company by the age of 23. When the Internet became a dominant player in the way consumers look for information, Tricia, was a premier National Speaker for Realtor.com, that educated real estate professionals on how to market their listings and get found online. Her success led her to creating corporate training programs for the national sales force at Realtor.com. Her combined experience of sales, management, marketing and direction has brought her the opportunity to speak for major brands including Century 21, Keller Williams, Prudential, Kodak, DS News, RIS media and more.

Since 2002, Andreassen has led Pro Step Marketing and Advertising, the leading strategy firm in the real estate industry as well as Pro Step Biz Marketing, which provides marketing services for small and medium size businesses, www.RealtyBizCoach.com which provides online study and marketing tools for real estate as well as Andreassen Coaching and Consulting which provides coaching programs and speaking services. She evangelizes the message of Interfusion Marketing®. This message has resulted in many top business leaders ranking in publications like the Wall Street Journal for their industries. They are following a proven method of success that Tricia has brought to their business. To learn more about Tricia Andreassen's systems and strategies or to book her for your next event please visit www.TriciaAndreassen.com or call 866-799-9888

www.facebook.com/LeadGenerationCoach

www.twitter.com/triciasings

www.linkedin.com/in/triciaandreassen

Get started now with your Interfusion Marketing strategy!

Access complimentary worksheets that you can use with this book as well as access to Tricia's marketing ideas and tips at www.InterfusionMarketingBook.com

Need help getting your creative ideas implemented or need one-on-one strategic coaching to pull it all together?

Real Estate:	www.ProStepMarketing.com
Self-Study Real Estate Courses:	www.RealtyBizCoach.com
Business Solutions:	www.ProStepBizMarketing.com
VIP Private Coaching:	www.TriciaAndreassen.com
Booking Tricia at Your Next Event:	www.TriciaAndreassen.com

For more information contact us at 1-866-799-9888 or email Info@InterfusionMarketingBook.com

1251 Hwy 16 North

Denver, NC 28037